BUDDHISM IN BRITAIN

Buddhism in Britain

IAN P. OLIVER

RIDER & COMPANY
LONDON

Rider & Company
3 Fitzroy Square, London W1P 6JD

An imprint of the Hutchinson Publishing Group

London Melbourne Sydney Auckland
Wellington Johannesburg and agencies
throughout the world

First published 1979
© Ian P. Oliver 1979

Set in Monotype Bembo

Printed in Great Britain by
The Anchor Press Ltd and bound by
Wm Brendon & Son Ltd, both of
Tiptree, Essex

British Library Cataloguing in Publication data
Oliver, Ian P.
    Buddhism in Britain.
    1. Buddhism – Great Britain – History
    I. Title
    294.3'0941   BQ709.G/

ISBN 0 09 138160 6 cased
       0 09 138161 4 paper

Dedicated to Carol, when I couldn't be with her, and to Christopher in the hope that he will grow up to live a life in the Dharma.

Contents

Acknowledgements		9
Foreword by Christmas Humphreys		11
Introduction		17

1 The Pali Text Society

The Pali Text Society	21
Professor T. W. Rhys Davids (1843–1922)	27

2 Some Early Buddhist Scholars and Pioneers

Mrs C. A. F. Rhys Davids (1858–1942)	35
Sir Edwin Arnold (1832–1904)	37
Max Muller (1823–1900)	39
Frank L. Woodward (1871–1952)	41
Ananda Metteyya Thera (1872–1923)	43
Dr Edward Conze (1904–)	45

3 The Buddhist Society

1924–1967	49
The last ten years	58

4 Flowers of Wisdom – the Theravada Tradition

The London Buddhist Vihara and the British Mahabodhi Society	65
The Buddhist Centre, Oaken Holt	74
The Buddhapadipa Temple	84
Shades of Dhamma	88
The British Buddhist Association	91
Addendum: Dhammapadipa (The Hampstead Buddhist Vihara)	101

5   **The Multi-Coloured Mandala – Tibet in Britain**
The Kagyu Samye-Ling Tibetan Centre   105
The Gyalwa Karmapa and the Kagyudpa lineage   108
Kham Tibetan House   115
The Manjushri Institute   129
The Four Great Meditations   142
The College of Tibetan Buddhist Studies   146
A Sense of Universal Responsibility: The XIVth Dalai
  Lama's Message to the West   151

6   **Friends of the Western Buddhist Order – a New
    Concept in Buddhism**
The FWBO Brighton, Amitayus   167
The FWBO Glasgow, Heruka   168
The FWBO Norwich, Vajradhatu and Vajrakula   169
Padmaloka   170
The FWBO London, Mandala and Ratnadvipa   171
Sukhavati   172
Golgonooza   173
Aryatara   173
The women's communities   175

7   **The Zen Buddhist Priesthood – Throssel Hole
    Priory**
The Soto Zen Priory of Throssel Hole   178
Ceremonials and services in the Soto Zen way   187

8   **Useful Information**
A Pali/Sanskrit/Japanese glossary   193
A Buddhist directory   203
Bibliography   216

Index   221

Acknowledgements

The author would like to express his acknowledgement to the following people without whose help this book would have been impossible:

Dr J. D. Dhirasekera, Editor-in-Chief, the *Encyclopedia of Buddhism*, Colombo, Sri Lanka; Mr Russell Webb and the Ven. H. Saddhatissa, The London Buddhist Vihara/British Mahabodhi Society, London; Miss I. B. Horner (President), Pali Text Society, London; Dr Edward Conze; Phra Khun Silananda, Senior Incumbent, Buddhapadipa Temple, London; Ven. Dr M. Vajiragnana, Religious Director, British Buddhist Association, London; Ven. Akong Tarap Rimpoche, Administrator, Kagyu Samye-Ling Tibetan Centre, Eskdalemuir, Scotland; Ven. Chime Rimpoche, Kham House, Saffron Walden; Mr Frank McAllen, Karma Kagyu Cho-Ling, London; Mr Roy Tyson (Secretary), The Manjushri Institute, Ulverston, Cumbria; Ven. Maha Sthavira Sangharakshita, Friends of the Western Buddhist Order, 'Padmaloka', Norwich and Upasakas Buddhadasa, Mangala, Devamitra, Kamalashila, Ajita, Vairocana, Kulananda, Nagabodhi, Vessantara and Upasika Anoma; Rev. Jisho Perry, Shasta Abbey, California, USA; Mr Maurice Walshe, Dhammapadipa, London; Mr Roy Brabant-Smith, Lay Buddhist Association, London; and lastly to Mr Christmas Humphreys for his invaluable advice throughout the compilation of the book, and especially for his Foreword.

I would also like to extend my acknowledgement to the following for their permission to use copyright material in the book: Mr Russell Webb and Ven. H. Saddhatissa – *A Buddhist's Manual*, and *Buddhist Quarterly*; Roshi Jiyu Kennett – *Zen is Eternal Life*; Rev. Jisho Perry – *Journal of Throssel Hole Priory*; HH Dalai Lama, Library of Tibetan Works and Archives – *The Universal Responsibility and the Good Heart*; John Murray (Publishers) Ltd, London – *The Dhammapada*, trans. Narada Thera; FWBO, Windhorse Press, Surrey – *Sayings, Poems, Reflections*, Ven. Sangharakshita.

Foreword

by Christmas Humphreys

Mr Oliver has asked me to write a Foreword to his careful survey of Buddhism in Britain, and its component schools and personalities. As I have spent some sixty years in this field, and taken part in some of its developments, I am happy to introduce this volume to the growing number of those who want help in finding their way about it.

It is not difficult to understand the fast rising interest in the subject, but 'Buddhism' is a very large term, with many meanings. It is a Western word which includes a wide variety of mental and spiritual culture, all developing from the Teaching of Gautama the Buddha who lived and taught in North-East India in the sixth century BC. The enormous literature of 'The Wisdom that has gone beyond', perhaps the high-water mark of human thought; its range of mysticism, philosophy and psychology; its powerful morality, and its beauty of culture and art, these at one time covered one third of the world in a wide variety of schools which had at their heart, none the less, the same deep spiritual principles. Why just three of these schools have established themselves in Great Britain is hard to say, but such is the position today.

In order of arrival they were the Theravada, the oldest existing school, found today in Sri Lanka, Thailand and Burma; Zen Buddhism, born in China but now best known in Japan; and Tibetan Buddhism. As I set out in detail in my *Sixty Years of Buddhism in England*, published in 1968, the first Buddhist missionary to preach Dhamma in England as a way of life of value to the Western mind was Ananda Metteyya, an Englishman who took this name when ordained as a Bhikkhu in the Theravada in Burma. This was in 1908, seventy years ago, and the Buddhist Society of Great Britain and Ireland was formed in London to prepare the way for his arrival. Ananda Metteyya died in London in 1923, and the present Buddhist Society was formed, as a lodge of the Theosophical Society, by my wife and myself in 1925, as it seemed that the original Society had not survived the war. Buddhism in England was then exclusively Theravada.

It was not until 1927, when the first volume of Dr D. T. Suzuki's *Essays in Zen Buddhism* appeared in London, that the existing Buddhist community, and the far wider circle of those interested in Eastern thought, learnt of the enormous range of Mahayana Buddhism in general and Zen Buddhism in particular. Here was something utterly new to the English spiritual horizon, although many of its principles had been firmly declared in *The Secret Doctrine* of H. P. Blavatsky some twenty years earlier. This epoch-making volume, and those which rapidly followed from the same source, opened the eyes of many to the width and depth and splendour of Buddhism, and provided a peaceful compliment to the moral philosophy of the Theravada.

After the war my legal duties took me to Japan, where I spent all my spare time with Dr Suzuki. On my return to England I worked as his European agent to publish and have republished further works of his on Zen Buddhism. These further prepared the way for his visits to England in the fifties, and soon it was clear that with the help of other books on the subject Zen Buddhism had come to stay.

In 1956 the World Fellowship of Buddhists, founded in 1950 by Dr Malalasekera, celebrated in New Delhi, as guests of the Indian Government, the 2500th anniversary of the Buddha's Enlightenment, and the Dalai Lama and the Panchen Lama flew down from Lhasa to attend. Three years later came the rape of Tibet which had the ironic effect that a large number of high-ranking Lamas who had escaped with the Dalai Lama were free to promulgate, in lectures, books and special schools, the profound wisdom and specialist techniques of Tibetan Buddhism. Soon a number of these came to London, led by the Venerable Thrungpa Rimpoche and Chime Rimpoche, and the first Tibetan Centre, that of Samye-Ling, was established near Dumfries in Scotland. More centres were opened in rapid succession, and Tibetan Buddhism put down its roots besides those of the Theravada in various parts of the country. Sinhalese and Thai viharas were opened near London together with Rinzai and Soto Zen centres. These three main schools of Buddhism had clearly come to stay.

Meanwhile the Buddhist Society, in its headquarters in Eccleston Square, near Victoria Station, was firmly established as the centre at which all Buddhist schools, and enquirers of all kinds and degree, were alike welcome, and where the unique tolerance found in every corner of the Buddhist world was well displayed. The Society adopted a long list of Buddhist groups which sprang up in all corners of the United Kingdom, and affiliated them to its own central organization, linked by personal visits and by its Journal, founded in 1926, the *Middle Way*. Then other purely British societies were founded, such as the Friends of the Western Buddhist Order, under the Ven. Sangharakshita, and the British Buddhist Association, founded by Mr Anthony de Haviland Nye. The climax to this crescendo of development came in June 1977, the 70th anniversary of Buddhism in England, when a leader of 'British Buddhism' was invited, as such, to the National Thanksgiving Service in St Paul's Cathedral for the Queen's Jubilee.

Of course the question is asked, why this welcome to a collection of strange doctrines from the East, and if the diminished interest in formal Christianity had created a religious void which the Western mind felt an increasing need to fill, why Buddhism? Why not Vedanta, or Taoism, or for that matter Islam? Mr Oliver has tried to answer these questions, and to describe the field of Buddhism as it appears in our midst today. Whether or not there will one day be a specifically

Western form of Buddhism is a further question which, if it cannot be lightly answered, at least gives rise to fascinating speculation. The Dhamma travelled far from its homeland in North-East India, and always, when it reached some country where it was later adopted by the local populace, the new religion cheerfully accepted some of the proven principles of the indigenous faith, thus producing yet another form or school of Buddhism which might on the surface differ from some other school created some hundreds or thousands of miles away. Hence, although the basic principles were ever the same, the outward appearance might differ widely, as with Theravada, Zen and Tibetan Buddhism.

What will happen in Britain? Will there be a blend of all these three, and others still arriving, adopting for use some of the basic principles of Christianity? Or will those who wish to follow the Buddhist Way choose for themselves one of the established forms of it? Time will tell, but meanwhile Mr Oliver has explored and described with great care the many schools and personalities in 'British Buddhism' today, surely proving to any reasonably minded and unbiased reader that Buddhism is here to stay, as a religion for those who feel the need for such and so regard it, and as a way of life for those who prefer that analogy.

My own view in brief is that none of these schools will develop very far as such, although each will have its centres for training and meditation, ritual or specific ceremonies. The main influence of Buddhism in the West will, in my view, be the absorption by Western philosophy, psychology, morality and even culture of those principles common to all its schools, apart from its own amazing tolerance of every differing point of view. The awareness of Totality, for example, in the Universe and in the human mind, the oneness of Life with its infinite forms, and the consequent compassion for every form of it, high or low, and the long Way to the reduction of selfish desire or egotism, which the Buddha claimed to be the cause of nearly all our suffering; all these within the ambit of total, living and intelligent LAW, manifesting in the twin doctrines of Karma and Rebirth, these I find are soaking into the Western mind and becoming fruitful within the doctrine that a man believes a doctrine when he behaves as if it were true.

Meanwhile, I have warned Mr Oliver that he is describing at one moment of time a state of afiairs which is moving very fast, and if the speed of development continues his book will need perpetual revision. Let us hope that Rider and Company who have given us such a wealth of books on Buddhism in the last thirty years will be, so far as the laws of publishing permit, sympathetic to this need.

Introduction

Throughout the West today we are undergoing an era of material and spiritual change. An era in which Christian ideals and values have lost their once revered authoritative splendour to the practical and dynamic Eastern and Oriental philosophies and religions. If we ask ourselves why this is so, it ultimately boils down to the fact that faith and belief in a theological divinity, which is as abstruse as the concept itself, is just not enough to satisfy totally those who are seeking first-hand *experience* of That which is the Reality deep within themselves, and is identical to the nature of the cosmos. In other words, the Oriental and Asian religions and philosophies give us Westerners that which rural Christianity cannot – existential experience. Meditation gives us this most necessary experience and inner tranquillity, this awakening, which faith in something, 'beyond and above ourselves' cannot.

Buddhism is one of those 'religions' which offer us this experience, hence the popularity of Buddhism in its many forms and schools in the West today. I would not put this popularity down to mass proselytism, much less Christian-styled evangelism. To look back in our history, books reveal that Buddhism, being the missionary 'religion' that it is, has never stopped growing in the past twenty-five centuries.

Although no one can pinpoint any particular date for the coming of Buddhism to the West, we can look back upon some of the leading scholars of the day and the work they carried out for the advancement of the Dharma. Some of the earliest publications came from the pens of such people as Burnouf and Lassen, who together gave us an essay on Pali in 1826. There were also George Turnour's translation of the *Mahavamsa* (1837) and Victor Fausboll's *Dhammapada* in 1885. Dr Herman Oldenburg presented to the Western world his voluminous *Vinaya-Pitaka*, which took the years between 1879 and 1883 to compile. A contemporary of the above named, Prof. T. W. Rhys Davids stood as one of the most remarkable figures in Western Buddhist history and in 1881, after his successful delivery of the *Hibbert Lectures*, paved the way for the founding of the Pali Text Society. However, two years prior to this saw the publication of a milestone in the annals of nineteenth-century Buddhist literature, namely Sir Edwin Arnold's beautiful verse account of the life of the Buddha, *The Light of Asia*.

Although these erudite men showed the way and gave the West a taste of Pali Buddhism in its pristine form, there still lacked a driving force to turn this idealistic philosophy into an experiential reality. This transformation was to become the work of an extraordinary man from London named Allan Bennett (Ananda Metteyya). In 1898 he entered Ceylon, proclaiming himself a self-converted Buddhist. Having later travelled to Burma to enter the Sangha, he vowed that he would return to spread the Buddha's teaching and to plant the seed of Dhamma in the West.

Meanwhile a society was formed to prepare the coming mission from Burma. Amongst the eminent Buddhists giving backing to this venture were Francis Payne, Dr Ernest Rost, R. J. Jackson and J. R. Pain. At a meeting in Harley Street there first came into being the Buddhist Society of Great Britain and Ireland, presided over by Prof. Rhys Davids with Prof. Edmund T. Mills, FRS, as Chairman, the year 1907.

So we had the beginnings of a new era, not only for Western man but also a new dimension to the already multi-dimensional spirit of Buddhism. Buddhism has never remained a static entity. It has continually wefted and weaved into so many diverse cultures throughout its history that it seemed the West would provide an insurmountable challenge to its indubitable doctrines. I believe it was Roshi Jiyu Kennett who once said that if Buddhism is to flourish in a foreign land, then it must be prepared to undergo admixtures of cultural traditions and domestic conventions but still retain its primordial teachings. Any readers who have dipped into the vast ocean of Buddhism will, I think, agree with my assumption.

The past ten years have seen a notable influx of Buddhist teachers which have prompted many to establish centres in their name and to proclaim their words of wisdom. The teachings contained in the Vajrayana of Tibetan Buddhism is rapidly taking root in the 'New Age' of spirituality reborn Truth-seekers. People are genuinely realizing the transformation which develops in one who sincerely puts into practice the teachings of Buddhism. And of course the vast collection of scriptures and commentaries continue to turn up on the bookshelves, inspiring one on his way.

Zen continues to grow with the emergence of the first Zen monastery to be established in Britain. Deep in the heart of Cumbria we have Throssel Hole Priory, a secluded retreat where the previously unknown teachings of Soto Zen are being offered. The Buddhist Society's Zen classes are also thriving under the care of Christmas Humphreys and Dr Irmgard Schloegl, herself an accredited teacher of Rinzai Zen.

With the return of Ven. Sangharakshita from his Vihara in Kalimpong in 1967, we now have a concretely established Western Buddhist Order. This movement engenders much of what is good and typical of Buddhism. Here we find tolerance for all points of view and a magnanimous spirit towards society – something chronically missing from twentieth-century life.

And the Theravadins, who have been such a mainstay in British Buddhist history. There was a time when one felt that the Mahayanistic euphoria which began sweeping through Buddhist circles in the early sixties would have completely undermined the previous seventy years of Theravadin prevalence. But this proved negative and in fact the Pali and Theravada form of Buddhism are on the increase again with the coming of such new centres as 'Oaken Holt' and the British Buddhist Association.

In Britain today, Buddhist groups and societies seem to be merging overnight and it is sometimes difficult, if not impossible, to gauge the exact number as a whole. The number of actual Buddhists practising and studying the Dharma in Britain is incalculable, and unless a census be taken, the exact number will remain beyond our grasp. However, quantity is ultimately inferior to quality, and it is the intensity and devotion to the Buddhadharma which really matters. What can be appreciated is that a large number of both old and young people are being attracted to the liberating doctrines of Buddhism.

As can be seen from the Contents, the author has limited his survey to what he believes to be the most reputed Buddhist organizations disseminating the Dharma in Britain today. Nevertheless, there are many other lesser, but by no means unexclusive Buddhist groups and societies, existing up and down the country, most of which I have listed in Chapter 8 under 'Buddhist Directory'. I hope with the appearance of their names in this book I will have offered some recompense for their grateful and abundant help whilst compiling this book.

1 The Pali Text Society

The fish trap exists because of the fish; once you've gotten the fish you can forget the trap. The rabbit snare exists because of the rabbit; once you've gotten the rabbit, you can forget the snare. Words exist because of meaning; once you've gotten the meaning, you can forget the words. Where can I find a man who has forgotten words so I can have a word with him!

CHUANG TZU

The Pali Text Society

The above axiom to me, sums up the whole philosophy and strategy behind the Pali Text Society, even although the paragraph was once uttered by one of China's most famous philosopher/poets. Words, in the form of suttas, stanzas and commentaries, have been handed down, searched out and acquired by a handful of Westerners in the latter half of the nineteenth century, which today has revealed the early teachings of Buddha, so much cherished by the Orient for over two thousand years. Several great scholars, such as Fausboll, Oldenberg, Cowell, Lassen, Burnouf and last but not least Professor Rhys Davids, are worthy of respect for the great perseverance and purposive resolve they showed in proclaiming to the world the Pali scriptures.

There is no doubt about the role played by Prof. Rhys Davids in making known to the West, what could only be called at that time, Pali Buddhism, or the teachings of Gautama the Buddha as found in the Pali Canon. Because he was the founder of the Pali Text Society, I found it necessary to include his full biography in this chapter, as many of the early struggles and frustrations in founding such an enterprise and the subsequent Pali translations he finished, are sympathetically presented.

Prof. Rhys Davids announced during one of his famous *Hibbert Lectures*, the foundation of a Pali Text Society, which he insisted was 'to render accessible to students the rich stores of the earliest Buddhist literature now lying unedited and practically unused in the various manuscripts scattered throughout the University and other Public Libraries of Europe'. It can be gleaned from this statement that the Society would endeavour to trace this literature and to translate the mountain of texts, for the benefit and edification of all those seriously interested in the teachings of Buddhism. He foresaw the publications of romanized editions of original Pali texts and translations of these texts, in the hope that a more lucid and etymologically precise understanding of what the Buddha said would be conveyed.

From its inception in 1881, the Society has worked hard to edit the whole Pali Tipitaka, the voluminous canonical work containing the three 'baskets' of the Buddha's doctrine, i.e., Book of the Discipline (Vinaya Pitaka); Book of the Discourses (Sutta Pitaka) and the Book of the Higher Doctrine (Abhidhamma Pitaka). An interesting observation made by Narada Thera is, that the three 'baskets' put together would be about eleven times the size of the Bible.

To give the reader an idea of the books which comprise the Tipitaka I have listed them in their corresponding categories below:

Vinaya Pitaka
  Vibhanga

	Parajika	Major Offences
	Pacittiya	Minor Offences
Khandaka	*Mahavagga*	Great Section
	Cullavagga	Short Section

Parivara   The Epitome of the Vinaya

*Sutta Pitaka**

Anguttara Nikaya	Collection of Discourses
Digha Nikaya	Collection of Long Discourses
Khuddaka Nikaya	Small Collection of Discourses
Majjhima Nikaya	Collection of Middle-length Discourses
Samyutta Nikaya	Collection of Kindred Sayings

The most popular of discourses to be found in the Sutta Pitaka are the following:

Dhammapada; Theragatha; Therigatha; Jataka; Buddhavamsa; Niddesa; Khuddaka; Udana; Hivuttaka; Suttanipata; Petavatthu; and the *Cariyapitaka Suttas.*

Abhidhamma Pitaka	This basket is divided into seven books and deals mainly with mental and material compositions, ethics and spiritual training

Dhammasangani	Classification of Dhammas
Vibhanga	The Book of Divisions
Katha-Vatthu	Points of Controversy
Puggala-Pannatti	Description of Individuals
Dhatu-Katha	Discussion with Reference to Elements
Yamaka	The Book of Pairs
Patthana	The Book of Relations

For those who would find the Pali translations too prosaic, the author advises the serious reader to get a copy of Narada Thera's *A Manual of Abhidhamma* (Abhidhammatha Sangaha), probably one of the best introductions to this absorbing subject.

The Society, a non-profit-making organization, is as old to

*This 'basket' not only comprises sayings of the Buddha, but includes also various discourses by some of his chief disciples, i.e., Ananda, Moggallana, etc.

the West as Buddhism is. Apart from the hundreds of translations which have occurred over the years, the Society ran
a series of twenty-three Journals from 1882 to 1927, which I
am afraid are now out of print. Membership, which has
fluctuated over the years, and which currently amounts to about
150, is confined primarily to Universities, Libraries, Buddhist
Societies and Learned scholars. The fact that the only educational establishment offering a course in Pali, that being the
British Buddhist Association – Working Men's College, is
proof that this valuable language is to a certain degree being
neglected in this country.

It goes without saying that an institution which relies totally
on book sales and in some cases, generous donations from
individuals, for its survival, will be limited to the output of
publications and research undertaken. Also, when you take
into account rising prices of paper, ink, materials and labour,
in other words inflation, one can begin to wonder at the
perpetual problems facing the Society. However, with its
brilliant and erudite President, Miss I. B. Horner, now enjoying
her eighteenth successful year in that post, the Society looks
quite financially stable and eagerly awaits its centenary.

The Society hasn't had the type of history that say, the
Buddhist Society has had, in that the Society's history has been
largely a slow process of Pali translations. Being a publishing
company, its development and setbacks, its achievements and
shortcomings have revolved around book sales and sponsorship
deals.

One of the recurring problems faced by the Society is the
demands on reprints of particular texts. If, for instance, a novel
publisher receives news that one of his famous war-time novels
is in demand, a reprint can be put into operation. A market
research team will do a survey and if the demand is strong
enough then they will go ahead with publication, investing
possibly thousands of pounds, knowing that the book will sell
and hence turn over a comfortable profit. The Pali Text
Society's problems are different. If they receive word from
various quarters that J. J. Jones's *Mahavastu Translation*, vol. 1

(1959), is in demand, incidentally priced at £7.00, the first problem which must be overcome is find the initial capital with which to have the book printed. The other problem is, will the demand for the book be satisfactory enough to ensure that the capital invested will be covered? It's not as if the book in question will be a million-seller!

To give the reader an added appreciation of the problem. In 1974 the demand for reprints, and one must remember that in most cases these books are classics in the field of Pali scholarship, ran into some twenty-seven volumes in the Text Series ranging from the *Cariyapitaka Commentary*, Ed. D. L. Barua (1939) to the *Vimanavatthu Commentary*, Ed. E. Hardy (1901). The dates of the first editions of these valuable translations will give the reader an idea why these two examples require reprints. Another problem met with, especially in the earlier translations, is that in the light of novel discoveries in grammar, concordance and etymology, a complete re-translation becomes necessary again requiring more funds to cover the costs.

The Pali Text Society will celebrate its centenary in four years' time, a vast achievement for an otherwise modest-sized institution. This accomplishment becomes even more staggering when you think that Prof. Rhys Davids, the founding President, only foresaw it lasting ten years! Its high scholastic standards have been upheld by past Presidents such as Mrs Rhys Davids, DLITT, MA (1922–42) whose writings spanned an incredible twenty-five books, although in some her work was confined to introduction, indexes and dual editorships with such eminent scholars as S. Z. Aung and G. Landsberg.

Mrs Rhys Davids was succeeded by W. H. D. Rouse, MA, DLITT, whose presidency lasted the years 1942–50. Of his career, he will be remembered for his *Index to the Jatakas* (1890) and the Text translation of the *Jina-Carita* (1905).

Following W. H. D. Rouse was W. Stede, PHD, who presided over the Society during the years 1950–58. His contribution to Pali studies and scholarship began with his edition of the *Culla-Niddesa* (1918): *Lexicographical Notes* (1919); *Padas of Thera and Theri-gatha* (1927) and his *Sumangala-*

Vilasina, vols. 1 and 2 (1931–2). He will probably be remembered for his contribution to the voluminous *Pali–English Dictionary* which he shared joint-editorship with Prof. Rhys Davids. In 1959 the current President took over, and to date has shown a resolute will in her work over the past forty or so years. I must personally confess she is a delightful and alert lady.

To digress just a little, I feel that the reader should be made aware of another interesting Pali project presently being undertaken in the West. This is the *Critical Pali Dictionary* (CPD) having its headquarters in Copenhagen. As the title would suggest the objective of this centre is the completion of an immense Pali–English Dictionary. This work began with two men, Helmer Smith from Sweden and Dines Anderson, a Dane, and saw the publication of the first Fascicle in 1924. Today, the work still continues and the number of scholars employed has greatly increased, including articles from Holland Germany, Sri Lanka, India and even Czechoslovakia.

The heart of this project is being centred at the Royal Danish Academy of Science and Letters which has international support by many eminent Pali scholars. The magnitude of this work can be gauged from the fact that in 1960, when the eleventh volume had been completed, the editors envisaged an incredible twenty-five years of work still to be undertaken before the final page would be finished.

Generous subventions have been derived from the Danish Government, the Carlsberg Fund, the Rask-Orsted Fund and the University Library of Copenhagen has opened its doors to the many researchers on the project.

At a conference in Copenhagen in September, 1958, it was decided that the work should continue in Copenhagen on an international basis. The supervisory committee, responsible for the translatory and other work being undertaken, were appointed at the 1958 meeting and comprise: L. Alsdorf (Hamburg), Miss I. B. Horner (London P T S), H. Hendrikson (Copenhagen), G. P. Malalasekera (Sri Lanka) and H. Humbach (Saarbrucken).

The Pali Text Society, as mentioned earlier celebrates its

centenary in four years' time. At present it would seem that as a *ne plus ultra*, the Society will have accomplished the incredible feat of having translated the full Pali Canon into English. But having said that, I must point out that there still remains a 'mountain' of commentaries and tikas awaiting translation. Even although these works could be assumed on face value to be of secondary importance, we must not lose sight of the fact that these texts still comprise relevantly valuable material in the *understanding* of the primary texts.

Professor T. W. Rhys Davids (1843–1922)*

Thomas William Rhys Davids was born on 12 May 1843 at Colchester. One may say that from about 1864 till his death on 27 December 1922 he devoted himself single-mindedly to the promotion of Indian and, in particular, of Pali studies. He accomplished an almost incredible amount both for the advancement of these studies and in laying firm and strong foundations for the continuance of his life-work in the years to come.

His father was a leading Congregational Minister with a gift both of patient enthusiasm and of illuminating what would be otherwise dry details, both of which were outstanding characteristics of his son. Rhys Davids went to school in Brighton (and always loved the sea) and gave up a good opening in the legal profession in order to go to the University of Breslau. Here he studied Sanskrit under Professor Stenzler and took the Degree of Ph D. Entering the Ceylon Civil Service in 1864, he soon acquired a working knowledge of Sinhalese and Tamil. A curious incident directed his interest, and hence much of his energy subsequently, to Buddhism. For when a case about the occupation of a village vihara came before him as a magistrate and a document was produced in court in evidence, it was found that no one present could read it. I was

*An abridged version of the biography of Prof. Rhys Davids as it is to appear in the *Encyclopedia of Buddhism* originally written by Miss I. B. Horner of the Pali Text Society.

once told, I do not know with how much veracity, that this document contained a quotation from the *Vinaya-pitaka* and it was this that aroused such a keen interest in Rhys Davids as to determine him to master this apparently unknown language. It was Pali. Later, in his 1881 *Hibbert Lectures*, he paid a deeply felt tribute to the dying monk, Yatramulle Unnanse who regularly came some distance on foot to teach him this language and Buddhism even more. Rhys Davids often spoke of this monk as 'the best man I ever knew' who had 'an indescribable attraction about him, a simplicity, a high-mindedness, that filled me with reverence' (*Hibbert Lectures*, 1881, p. 187).

Pali, however, was not entirely unknown to the Western world. Eugene Burnouf with Professor Lassen had written an *Essay on Pali* in 1826; George Turnour, also of the Ceylon Civil Service, had published his combined edition and translation of the *Mahavamsa* in 1837 – a work which Rhys Davids called 'the foundation of all Pali Scholarship'; and R. C. Childers (who left Ceylon in 1864) had begun his *Dictionary of the Pali Language*, published in two volumes in 1872, 1875. Rhys Davids later appraised this as a 'great and important work – not only the most valuable contribution yet made to the study of that language [Pali], but the indispensable means by which further progress could be made'. It was reserved for Rhys Davids to bring some kind of organization to Pali studies in the West, to pave the way for Buddhism to become a household word, and to show its value as part of special knowledge and its mental or 'religious' significance to mankind as a whole.

Rhys Davids's earliest book was on *The Ancient Coins and Measures of Ceylon*, 1877. In 1878 there appeared his little manual on *Buddhism*, published by the Society for Promoting Christian Knowledge in its Non-Christian Religions Series. The 23rd edition was published in 1914. This book, founded on all Pali material then available concerning the Life and Teachings of the Buddha, contains also short sketches of the history of the Order and of the Tipitaka. Though only the modicum of canonical texts was accessible to him, the writer's extraordinarily clear insight is shown here time and time again as it was to be later, often as 'leaps in the Dark', in his writings and footnotes. His intellect took him straight to the heart of a matter, and having seen so far, nothing but the best on that subject was possible. In this book he stressed that Nibbana does not mean annihilation in the sense so often assigned to it, but signifies a moral and mental condition to be reached here in this world and in this life (see p. 110ff) and is, in fact, 'a changed state of mind' (*Hibbert Lectures*, 1881, Appendix X).

His reputation now brought him into correspondence with an increasing number of scholars, and opportunities of interpreting Buddhism were multiplied. His translation of the *Jataka Nidanakatha*, with its elaborate highly important and far-seeing introduction on the history of the Birth-Story literature and so forth was published in 1880 under the title *Buddhist Birth – Stories or Jataka Tales*. It may be regarded as the preamble to the translation of Fausboll's *Jataka*, issued under the editorship of Professor E. B. Cowell in six volumes (Cambridge University Press, 1895–1907).

The next year, 1881, was to prove extremely productive and memorable. It saw Rhys Davids's first contribution to the *Sacred Books of the East*, a series of which Professor Max Muller was the editor, namely *Buddhist Suttas*, translated from the Pali (vol. 11). Moreover, in 1881–5, there appeared in this same series the three volumes entitled *Vinaya Texts* (vols. 13, 17, 20) which Rhys Davids had translated from the Pali in co-operation with Hermann Oldenberg. These works were followed in 1890, 1894 by *The Questions of King Milinda* (SBE vols. 35, 36, reprinted in the USA in 1965). In his estimation the text of the Milindapanha was 'the masterpiece of Indian prose'. His two Introductions, one to each volume, are immensely valuable and may be read with great profit even today.

This same year, 1881, was also the year in which Rhys Davids delivered his six justly famous *Hibbert Lectures*. In the second of these he was able to announce the foundations of the Pali Text Society, the avowed object of which was, in his own words, 'to render accessible to students the rich stores of the earliest Buddhist literature now lying unedited and practically unused in the various MSS. scattered throughout the University and other Public Libraries of Europe'. A group of distinguished scholars in Ceylon, Burma, England, France, Germany, Holland and the United States had welcomed the project, and the first Committee of the Pali Text Society contained the honoured names of Victor Fausboll, Hermann Oldenberg, Richard Morris and Emile Senart with Rhys Davids as Chairman. Rhys Davids had an excellent business head and a power of interesting influential people, and since his knowledge of what he wanted was clear and exact he was able to convince them and enlist their support.

After the Society had been successfully launched and the original plan of editing the texts in roman characters had developed well, Rhys Davids was able to enlarge the sphere of publication, in accordance with his original conception, so as to include translations. Professor Max Muller encouraged him to inaugurate *The Sacred Books of the Buddhists* on the closure of the *Sacred Books of the East*. The first two volumes in this new series were published in 1895, 1899 under the gracious patronage of HM King Chulalongkorn, King of Siam, and the next two under that of his successor. This series now (1966) contains twenty-five volumes. The Translation Series was begun in 1909, as an addition to the *Sacred Books of the Buddhists*. It now contains thirty-two volumes.

Realizing too that his friend Childers's *Dictionary of the Pali Language* (1872, 1875) was becoming out of date, Rhys Davids turned his thoughts to a new *Pali–English Dictionary*, and in his inter-leaved copy of Childers's *Dictionary* (now in my possession) he noted every new word, illustrative passage and unusual grammatical construction that came to light as more and more Pali texts were edited in roman characters.

But this most cherished of all his ambitions which in 1908, he had hoped to place on an international footing, was doomed to frustrating delays. Scholars in other lands beset by the hazards of academic life, found it not always possible to keep their promises of collecting material, and, with the outbreak of war in 1914, the project had to be not so much abandoned, as shouldered entirely by its instigator. However, in 1921 the Pali Text Society 'after long-continued exertion and many cruel rebuffs and disappointments, is now at last in a position to offer scholars the first instalment of the new Dictionary'. For this Rhys Davids had collected £2160 from a variety of donors (including H M the King of Siam, £500) in many parts of the world. In his Foreword to Part I of the *Pali–English Dictionary* he wrote, 'The work is essentially preliminary . . . to wait for perfection would postpone the much-needed dictionary. It has therefore been decided to proceed as rapidly as possible with the completion of this first edition, and to reserve the proceeds of the sale for the eventual issue of a second edition which shall come nearer to our ideals of what a Pali Dictionary should be.' Though the eventual second edition is still only a distant vision, the original edition remains an invaluable tool and has been reprinted several times.

In 1882 Rhys Davids became Professor of Pali in University College, London – an honorary post, and soon afterwards, as Secretary and Librarian of the Royal Asiatic Society (1885–1904). His labours were added to at the same time by his share in founding both the British Academy and the School of Oriental Studies (now the School of Oriental and African Studies) and by his efforts to inaugurate an Indian Texts Series.

Yet his own scholarly work continued unabated. In 1884 the Pali Text Society published his careful edition of Anuruddha Thera's *Abhidhammatthasangaha* in its Journal, and in 1886 there appeared the first volume of the *Sumangalavilasini*, edited by Rhys Davids in collaboration with his friend, Professor J. Estlin Carpenter. In 1890, 1911 the same two friends edited the *Digha-nikaya*, vols. I and II. The importance of the *Digha* had been eloquently stressed in the Introduction to the *Sumangalavilasini*, vol. I. Here too are laid down certain principles which Pali Text Society editors still strive to follow.

Such an amount of heavy and important work, including

the mass of correspondence it entailed, might well have over-
whelmed another man – he suffered also recurrent bouts of
malaria contracted in Ceylon. But in 1894 his power was
doubled by his marriage with Augusta Caroline Foley, whose
largeness of heart and brain, disciplined intellect and unbounded
energy made her a fit partner in so full a life. There were three
children of the marriage, two daughters and a son whose life
of brilliant promise was sacrificed in the Air Force of 1917.

Soon after their marriage Rhys Davids went to America to
deliver lectures at Cornell University, 1894–5. These were
published under the title *Buddhism: Its History and Literature*
(New York, 1896). In 1899 he had the great happiness of a visit
to India and the Buddhist historical sites. One of the results of
this journey was his remarkable book on *Buddhist India* (1903,
8th ed., 1959).

It is to be regretted that the other and more ambitious scheme
that emerged from his visit to India came to life only with
difficulty in spite of the approval and active interest of that
eminent man of culture, Lord Curzon, then Viceroy at Calcutta. This was the Indian Texts Series (already referred to),
the purpose of which was to furnish full and accurate materials
for the study of the history of India.

In 1904 Rhys Davids was appointed Professor of Comparative Religion in the Victoria University of Manchester. It was
a new post, indeed the first university post created in England
for this subject. Here, till he retired in 1915, he lectured on
almost the whole field of the history of religion except that of
Greece and Rome which was in the hands of the Professors of
Classics. Though so replete with learning and erudition, he
was never the 'dry' scholar or pedant. In sharing his knowledge
with his pupils and subordinating his own part so as to give
value to their efforts, he inspired some of them with his own
ardour, delighted in their advance, and was never happier than
in helping them over difficulties and enlisting their aid. This
was at the root of, for example, his venture to produce a
Pali–English Dictionary that would be more up-to-date than
Childers's (for which he had nothing but the highest admiration)

and of his hope that this in its turn would be superseded one day by an improved second edition.

In 1910 and 1921 he completed, with the collaboration of Mrs Rhys Davids, the translation of the *Digha-nikaya*, called *Dialogues of the Buddha*, published in the Sacred Books of the Buddhists, of which he had translated the first volume alone (1899). It is here perhaps that, as an expositor of early Buddhism Rhys Davids was at his best.

In 1910 the newly formed India Society (now the Royal India Pakistan and Ceylon Society) made him their President. Attendance at its Council Meetings and at those of the British Academy which induced him to take the long fatiguing journeys between London and Manchester, grew to be sorely irksome to him. So, full of years and academic honours, he decided to leave Manchester and in 1915 settled in Chipstead, Surrey. Here he lived a quiet scholar's life, often suffering much pain, but working through it and not, till near the end, giving up the golf and other games, outdoor and indoor, which had been his refreshment for so long. As has been said already, the great work of his last years was, with the steady and reliable help of Dr W. Stede, the final arranging of the material for the new *Pali–English Dictionary*. One can only rejoice that about a third of it had been published and issued to subscribers when hypostatic pneumonia supervened upon his other maladies, and, after two days of suffering, he passed peacefully away.

In all that he did, Rhys Davids bore the stamp of complete integrity of thought and character. His very great erudition never sat heavily on him. In conversation he was learned, brilliant, and of entrancing interest, but yet people who knew him remember well how the humour that constantly came bubbling out of him, enlivening everything, made his deep wisdom palatable.

Knowledge for Rhys Davids was not a mere accumulation of facts or theories. What he desired was the living voice of all ages. 'For,' he said, 'that knowledge of what man has been in distant times, in far-off lands, under the influence of ideas which at first sight seem to us so strange, will strengthen within

B

us that reverence, sympathy and love which must follow on a realization of the mysterious complexity of being, past, present and to come, that is wrapped up in every human life.' That reverence, sympathy and love was the mainspring of his work and brought him to a deep understanding of the Teachings of the Buddha. 'Buddhist or not Buddhist,' he wrote, 'I have examined every one of the great religious systems of the world, and in none of them have I found anything to surpass in beauty and comprehensiveness, the Noble Eightfold Path of the Buddha. I am content to shape my life according to that Path.'

2 Some Early Buddhist Scholars and Pioneers

Mrs C. A. F. Rhys Davids (1858–1942)

Mrs Rhys Davids probably still stands as one of the most brilliant expositors and translators of Pali Buddhism in British Buddhist history. Being the wife of the great Prof. T. W. Rhys Davids, she showed an incisive intellect in her early Pali studies, and later in her own scholastic translations.

She was born in 1858 as Caroline Augusta Foley and had a extraordinary primary and secondary career leading up to her entrance to University College in London. She graduated M A and D Lit, later being elected a Fellow of the university. The interest she showed in languages, literature and oriental studies saw her become Reader in Pali at the London School of Oriental and African Studies. Later in her career, she took up the post of Lecturer in Indian Philosophy at Manchester University.

At the age of thirty-six, she married Thomas William Rhys Davids, who was a young fifty-two-year-old – the year, 1894. The fact that both had similar academic interests and backgrounds, and that both were uncannily individualistic, proved paradoxically enough the very qualities which kept them close and devoted to each other. They had a perfectly happy marriage. Their marriage produced two daughters and a son. Unfortunately their only son was killed in action during the First World War in 1917. This became a great loss to the family.

The authority she showed in her Pali work came to fruition when she was appointed President of the Pali Text Society in 1922, a post she held with utmost perfection for twenty years.

Always a prolific scholar and writer, and not always assenting to the authenticity of previous works by earlier Pali scholars she exhibited her own unique and interpretative renderings of difficult Pali texts.

The long list of translations and associated works stands the test of time, that here was a peerless individual who dedicated half her life to the presentation of Pali Buddhism to the world. The list of her translations and Romanized texts make impressive reading:*

The Dhammasangani (Buddhist Psychological Ethics)	1900
The Earliest Rock Climb	1901
The Vibhanga, edited by Mrs Rhys Davids	1904
The Duka-patthana, edited by Mrs Rhys Davids	1906
Studies in the Nikayas	1907–8
Psalms of the Sisters (Therigatha)	1909
Abhidhammatha-Sangaha (Compendium of Philosophy). Ed. with S. Z. Aung	1910
The Digha Nikaya (Dialogues of the Buddha), Vol. II with Prof. Rhys Davids	1910
The Yamaka, Vol. I	1911
The Yamaka, Vol. II	1913
The Kathavatthu (Points of Controversy), with S. Z. Aung	1915
Samyutta-Nikaya (The Book of the Kindred Sayings), Vol. I	1917
Visuddhimagga, Vol. I	1920
Visuddhimagga, Vol. II	1921
Samyutta-Nikaya, Vol. II	1921
Tikapatthana and Commentary, Vol. I	1922
Tikapatthana and Commentary, Vol. II	1922
Tikapatthana and Commentary, Vol. III	1923
A Milestone in Pali Text Society Work	1923
Majjhima-Nikaya, Vol. IV (indexes)	1925
Buddhism and the Negative	1927

*All books published by Pali Text Society: see Chapter 8.

Minor Anthologies: Vol. I *Dhammapada*; *Khuddakapatha*;
   Text and Translation   1931
Psalms of the Brethren (Theragatha), 2nd ed.   1937

Also, *Gotama the Man* ⎫
    Sakya or Buddhist Origins ⎬ all dates unknown to author
    Wayfarers Words ⎭

Sir Edwin Arnold (1832–1904)

Edwin Arnold was born on 10 July 1832 at Gravesend, Kent. In his youth he attended Kings School, Rochester and later Kings College, London. During his academic career at Kings, he won a scholarship which gave him entrance to University College, Oxford, a 'kindergarten' for politicians, poets, scientists and philosophers.

His standing as a poet/author was evinced way back in 1852, when he won the Newdigate Prize for literature with his first poem called *The Feast of the Belshazzar*. The customary procedure at the university was that he should recite his prize-winning poem when the new Chancellor of the university was installed. This he did – the incumbent Chancellor being Lord Derby.

In 1853 he had his first book of poems published. They were *Poems Narrative and Lyrical* a brilliant anthology of beautiful English verse. Throughout the book, the influence of John Keats, the eighteenth-century English poet is much in evidence. He acquired the exclusive reputation of being the second layman in history, next to Max Muller, to address the congregation of Westminster Abbey.

In 1854, at the age of twenty-two, he married Katherine Biddulph. After graduating M A from Oxford, he took up the post of Master at King Edward V I School in Birmingham, resigning three years later to take up an assignment as Principal of Deccan College at Poona in India. This move gave Arnold the ideal opportunity to study Eastern religion and culture, which was an intangible theme in his later writings. In the second half of the 1800s and after mastering the Sanskrit language, he wrote various books and translations from the Sanskrit originals which included a two-volume history of the political administration of Lord Dalhousie.

After replying to a newspaper advertisement in the *Daily Telegraph*, he was eventually chosen as a correspondent in Asian affairs, in 1861. His dedication to the paper saw him promoted to Editor. He worked for the paper both at home and abroad for forty years.

The Light of Asia, one of the most popular and pastoral compositions of the life story of Gautama ever written, was conceived in the 1870s, much of it being jotted down in his spare time and written at Hamlet House, Southend. It soon became a particular quirk of Edwin, to all of a sudden write down, using the first piece of paper at hand, several inspirational lines, anywhere and at any time. The book was published in 1870 and almost immediately drew gasps of amazement at its poetic beauty, and today remains a revered book not only in the West but in the East.

The respect and courtesy offered to him, not only for his brilliant treatise on the life of Buddha, but as an innovator in East–West concord and amity can be witnessed in this tribute paid to him by the Ven. Weligama Sri Sumangala, head of the Vihara and College at Panadure, Ceylon:

You, meritorious and accomplished Sir, who have eclipsed the fame of other learned men as a mountain of diamonds would the lustre of mountains of other precious stones. Though born in a distant land, blessed with neither the religion of Sri Sakhya Muni of Solar Dynasty, the Most Holy Subduer of all desires, and World Honoured Conqueror of all evil passions, nor the intercourse of His devotees, have written in your own native language an elegant poem on His most holy and incomparable life, a poem embracing the close of His metempsychosical sojourn, as a noble Bodhisat in Tusitha Heaven. And the attainment of the Four Noble Truths, great and holy, a poem agreeing to the very letter, and disagreeing in no respect with all the other popular Buddhistical Scriptures, the Canon and the commentaries. And you have thereby accomplished a task which no English Pundit has hitherto wrought.

You alone, therefore, of all the English Scholars, are entitled to our loving praise.*

He was honoured twice in his life as a Companion of the (Order of the) Star of India, CSI, and also had conferred on him by the King of Siam the Order of the White Elephant in recognition of his services to Buddhism.

A pioneer in the struggle to have Buddhagaya restored to Buddhist hands, Arnold made full use of his newspaper connections in outlining his reasons. In 1889 he travelled as far as Japan to win over the Japanese, whose aid and influence he sought in his conquest. This noble mission was taken up many years later by the Anagarika Dharmapala in whose hands the ownership of Buddhagaya was decided.

Sir Edwin Arnold was brought up in a Christian country, dedicated to Christian values and dogmatics, and although he never publicly declared that he was in fact a Buddhist, the evidence that he voluntarily gave up the sport of shooting animals and birds would suggest that his moral commitment to Buddhist morality motivated him in the latter part of his life. He was knighted by Queen Victoria for his outstanding services both to Great Britain and to India. He died in March 1904.

Contributions to Indian, Sanskrit and Buddhist literature add up to the following:

The Light of Asia or (The Great Renunciation), published by Trübner & Co., 1879
The Song Celestial, or the Bhagavad-Gita
The Secret of Death
Indian Idylls (from the Sanskrit of the Mahabhavata)
Pearls of the Faith or, Islams Rosary
Indian Poetry (Oriental poems containing 'The Indian Song of Songs')
India Revisited (Sojourns in India and Ceylon), 1886

Max Muller (1823–1900)

Friedrich Max Muller was born on 6 December 1823, in the Duchy of Anhalt-Dessau in Germany. He was the son of

*India Revisited, Trübner & Co., London, 1886, page 268.

Wilhelm Muller, an eminent poet of the day. His father was a notable character himself, being a classical philologist, he became director of the local library and was an authority on Western languages. This characteristic could be seen in his son at an early age.

His father died at the age of thirty-three, leaving Max under the close care of his friend and confidant, Dr Carus. Max was next taken to Leipzig where Dr Carus guided his intellectual growth and learning. Although the young intellectual showed an exceptional virtuosity in music, he was advised by the composer Felix Mendelssohn that a career in philology would be more rewarding and would prove a greater challenge to his already intellectual genius.

Entering Leipzig University at seventeen, he graduated three years later with a Doctorate of Philology; a promising career was by now prophesied. The philosophical erudition of Schopenhauer impressed and influenced his own thought and studies. In 1844, his first book was published in German, being a translation from the Sanskrit of the classical *Hitopadesa*.

Two years later he went to Paris, a 'breeding ground' for up-and-coming Indologists, where he met and subsequently became a loyal pupil of the great French Buddhist translator and scholar Eugene Burnouf. Burnouf introduced Max to Vedantic philosophy and Buddhist doctrine, a turning point in his religious and literary studies. The influence and inspiration derived from Burnouf found expression in his project to edit the massive Indian classic the *Rigveda*. The money required to sponsor such a project was donated by the East India Company.

He set up home in England in 1848, with the main aim of being closer to the Sanskrit manuscripts of the *Rigveda* in London. Professor Wilson of Oxford, influenced Muller to take up residence in the university town, seeing the importance of being near valuable university libraries which held material relevant to his research. A year later, in 1849, the first of six volumes on the *Rigveda* was published, which, on that account, led to several special appointments in universities throughout

Britain. Firstly came the Taylorian Professorship of Modern European Languages in 1854; Curator of the Bodleian Library in 1856 and Fellow of All Souls College in 1858.

In 1860, he was appointed Professor of Philology at Christ Church, a post he held until his death in 1900.

Meanwhile, throughout all those years he dedicated himself to the momentous task of editing the epic *Rigveda*, a six-volume masterpiece spanning twenty-five years. Of course, Max Muller will also be renowned for his editorship of the *Sacred Books of the East*, an unparalleled anthology of Buddhist texts.

His authority in Indology was never disputed and was held in great esteem both in Britain and abroad. Probably the pinnacle of his brilliant academic career came when, at the invitation of Dean Stanley, he was asked to address the congregation of Westminster Abbey on religion, the first ever layman in history to do so. In his later career he acquired the respect and acclaim of fellow Indologists as being the greatest living authority on Indian religion as well as Buddhist philosophy.

Frank L. Woodward (1871–1952)

Frank L. Woodward was another originator of Pali studies in the nineteenth century. He was born the third son of the Rev. W. Woodward at Saham, Norfolk in 1871. Like many of his schoolboy contemporaries, he enjoyed a first-class education, specializing in languages, particularly German, French and Greek.

At the age of eighteen he entered Sidney Sussex College, Cambridge, winning a first classical scholarship and later, at nineteen, won a Gold Medal in Latin. He was by this time, a master of European languages and a philological career was pending after completion of university. In the third and last year of university he passed the Classical Tripos with Honours, a difficult degree to acquire.

His first professional post was assistant master at Rugby Preparatory School. In 1897 he left Rugby and went to the

Royal Grammar School, Worcester, as a classical master. It was during those years that he began the study of philosophy and the 'Buddhist' language of Pali, along with Sanskrit. This led to his joining the Theosophical Society where he became deeply impressd with Buddhism. Through the then President of the Society, Col. H. S. Olcott, he applied for a job in Ceylon which he subsequently gained, as headmaster of Mahinda College in Galle.

After a couple of years in Ceylon, his academic brilliance in the field of education soon won him respect and credibility sometimes reserved for learned Theras. In his sixteen years at Galle he not only educated youngsters but educated himself – spiritually. Like most Buddhists in Ceylon, he was a vegetarian and found the peace and contentment of solitude one of the most important possessions of his later life. Being liberal with educational expenses throughout his rectorship at Galle, his own private life was lived only slightly less frugally than that of a Buddhist monk.

In October of 1919, he left Galle for Tasmania where he dedicated the rest of his life to Pali Text translations.

His contributions to the literature are:*

Manual of a Mystic (Yogavacara's Manual), Appendix by D. B. Jayatilaka	1916
The Book of Kindred Sayings (Samyutta-Nikaya), Vol. III	1924
Some Sayings of the Buddha	1925
Udana Commentary	1926
The Book of Kindred Sayings (Samyutta-Nikaya), Vol. IV	1927
Saratthappakasini, Vol. I	1929
The Book of Kindred Sayings (Samyutta-Nikaya), Vol. V	1930
Saratthappakasini, Vol. II	1932
The Book of Gradual Sayings (Anguttara-Nikaya), Vol. I	1932
The Book of Gradual Sayings (Anguttara-Nikaya), Vol. II	1933
Minor Anthologies: Vol. II Udana: Verses and Uplift and Itivittaka: As it was said	1935
The Book of Gradual Sayings (Anguttara-Nikaya), Vol. V	1936
Saratthappakasini, Vol. III	1937

*Except *Some Sayings of the Buddha*, all published by Pali Text Society.

Theragata Commentary, Vol. I	1940
Theragata Commentary, Vol. II	1952
Theragata Commentary, Vol. III	1959

Although a master of the Pali language and an equally brilliant scholar, Frank L. Woodward will probably be remembered most for his comprehensive anthology, *Some Sayings of the Buddha*, his greatest contribution to Buddhism.

Ananda Metteyya Thera (1872–1923)

For as much as Ananda Metteyya did for Buddhism in England at the turn of the century, it is still surprising just how few people know of his existence. Apart from being the second Englishman to be ordained into the Sangha, it was he who led a very successful Buddhist Mission from Burma in 1908. Although Buddhism had been known in Britain for some thirty years previously, it was Ananda Metteyya who injected a practical dimension, which had hitherto been lacking and had the effect of inspiring more to 'come and see'.

Charles Henry Allan Bennett was born in London on 8 December 1872. He was the son of an engineer and, clearly impressed by his father's profession, studied science himself. During those early years he stumbled against a copy of Edwin Arnold's *The Light of Asia* which he consequently read; the impression upon his mind being incalculable. He diligently betook himself to the study of Buddhism whereupon, in 1898, he left for Ceylon with intentions of entering the Order. Whilst in Ceylon, Bennett further studied the Dhamma which led to his first lecture, delivered in 1901, entitled 'The Four Noble Truths'.

Bennett left for Burma that same year where, at Akyab in the state of Arakan, he became ordained Ananda Maitreya.* His first 'mission' was now completed, it only remained to commence the 'real' mission, one which would take him back to the land of his birth and to set 'the wheel of the law' in

*See page 49.

motion in the West. But before this, he founded in 1903, the Buddhasasana Samagama, or the International Buddhist Society, an immense undertaking aimed at the total consociation of Buddhists throughout the world. The Society had Ananda Metteyya as Secretary-General, with Dr E. R. Rost as Hon. Secretary. Running concurrently to this was an illustrated journal called *Buddhism* which had as its aim the spreading of the Buddhadhamma in the West, but particularly in Britain.

It was in this journal that the projected mission to the West was made public. In April of 1908, at the age of thirty-six, Ananda Metteyya set foot in England, welcomed by members of the Buddhist Society of Great Britain and Ireland. During his first visit the volume of work carried out by him was phenomenal, even although being chronically beset with asthma. He met, talked, corresponded with and initiated into Buddhism, many people and engendered an inspiration by his mere presence.

In October of 1908, Ananda Metteyya returned to Burma with Dr Rost to carry on his work in Rangoon delighted with his mission and the impact it had on Buddhism in England throughout his too short a stay. Back in Burma he resumed his work with *Buddhism* and also found time to submit short articles to *The Buddhist Review*, the Journal of the Buddhist Society.

Ananda Metteyya returned to Britain twice, firstly in 1914 whilst on a trip to the USA, but his ill-health on that occasion prevented him from attempting the long journey. And secondly in 1920, he came to London on a visit and delivered one lecture and became part Editor of the Buddhist Society's *Buddhist Review*.

Although of inspiring appearance and tranquil demeanour, Ananda Metteyya, according to several reports, was an unpolished speaker, a relative hindrance to one whose volume of missionary work and correspondence adequately made up for his oratory shortcomings. To a certain extent, it was he who was responsible for the conception and birth of the Buddhist Society as we know it today.

On 9 March, 1923, Ananda Metteyya died – he was fifty years old. During his life all his writings were concentrated in articles for journals and various lectures delivered both in the East and West. However, two months before he passed away, he saw the one and only ever full-length book published. *The Wisdom of the Aryas* was published by Kegan Paul, and was a compendium of papers written by him between 1917 and 1918. In this book was Metteyya's own personal dissertation on the Buddhadhamma, a unique work from a unique man.

Dr Edward Conze (1904–   )

Within the field of Mahayana Buddhism, there are few men, especially in the West, who have scaled those elevated heights of the Prajnaparamita sutras, or, 'the perfection of wisdom'. Indeed if there are, few would have the temerity to admit it. To me, and I think I speak for the majority of Western Buddhists, Dr Conze is one of those rare exceptions. No other man this century has applied himself so assiduously and skilfully to the study and exposition of Indian Mahayana Buddhism.

Edward Julius Dietrich Conze was born in London on March 18th, 1904 but left England for Germany where all his early schooling was undertaken. After his secondary education was completed at the German Gymnasia of Cologne and Düsseldorf from 1914 to 1922, he went on to study philosophy at the Universities of Tuebingen, Heidelberg, Kiel and Cologne. In 1928, he graduated PhD from Cologne University whereupon he continued further study in Indian and European comparative philosophy at the Universities of Bonn and Hamburg as a post-graduate. During these years (1928–33) he struck up a close working relationship with that most distinguished scholar Prof. E. Cassirer.

In 1933, after his post-graduate work in Hamburg, Dr Conze returned to England where he soon commenced extramural work at London and Oxford universities, taking Tutorial Classes in psychology and comparative religion.

This particular phase in his professional life came to a close in 1960. In his early youth, however, Dr Conze had already begun the study of Buddhism and the respective languages pertaining to the manifold sutras and commentaries extant. Throughout the Western world there were literally thousands of manuscripts awaiting translation, and to do justice to this rare and exceptionally deep accumulation of literature required an outstanding mind. And so Dr Conze's vocation arose – to translate the vast collection of Sanskrit and Tibetan Buddhist literature.

His first major contribution to Buddhist studies came in the form of his *Buddhism, Its Essence and Development* (1951) which preceded his joint editorship of *Buddhist Texts through the Ages* (1954) in collaboration with Arthur Waley, Miss I. B. Horner and D. L. Snellgrove. His translatory career got under way in 1954 with his translation from the Tibetan-Sanskrit original of the *Abhisamayalankara*, itself a commentary on the Prajna-paramita ascribed to Maitryanatha.

After 1954, Dr Conze resolutely dedicated himself to the scriptural study and translation of other major Mahayana sutras, especially the voluminous Prajnaparamita sutras. From this initial commitment came a profusion of classics so philo-logically and etymologically precise that paved the way for his recognition by so many leading Buddhists as a world authority on the subject. He saw in the Mahayana the culmination of all Buddhist philosophical and psychological thought and the flowering of the highest ideals which the human mind could conceive. His book publications since 1955 onwards contain so much literary artistry, not to mention authoritative splen-dour, that to commentate at length on them would result in the addition of another hundred pages to this chapter. Hence, the author sincerely hopes that the following bibliography will suffice in giving the reader a fragmentary glimpse of the direction in which his scholarly efforts have been channelled.

Selected Sayings from the Perfection of Wisdom (Buddhist
    Society, London – 133pp.)   1955
The Buddha's Law Among the Birds, translated from the
    Tibetan (B. Cassirer, Oxford – 65pp.)   1956

Buddhist Meditation (Allen and Unwin, London – 183pp.)   1956
Vajracchedika Prajnaparamita, edited and translated
 (Serie Orientale Roma – 114pp.)   1957
Astasahasrika Prajnaparamita – translated, *The Perfection
 of Wisdom in 800 Slokas* (The Asiatic Society, Calcutta
 – 225pp.)   1958
Buddhist Wisdom Books, *The Diamond Sutra* and *The
 Heart Sutra* (Allen and Unwin, London – 110pp.)   1958
Buddhist Scriptures (Penguin Classics – 250pp.)   1959
The Prajnaparamita Literature (Indo-Iranian Monographs
 no. VI, Mouton and Co., 's-Gravenhage – 123pp.)   1960
A Short History of Buddhism (Chetana Ltd, Bombay –
 117pp.)   1961
The Large Sutra on Perfect Wisdom, with divisions of the
 Abhisamayalankara Pt 1 (Luzac and Co., London –
 203pp.)   1961
*The Gilgit Manuscript of the Astadasasahasrika Prajnapara-
 mita*, ch. 55 to 70, edited and translated (Serie Orien-
 tale Roma – 390pp.)   1962
*Buddhist Thought in India, Three Phases of Buddhist
 Philosophy* (Allen and Unwin, London – 302pp.)   1962
Materials for a Dictionary of the Prajnaparamita Literature
 (Suzuki Research Foundation, Tokyo – 447pp.)   1967
Thirty Years of Buddhist Studies (B. Cassirer, Oxford –
 274pp.)   1968
*The Perfection of Wisdom in Eight Thousand Lines and its
 Verse Commentary* (Four Seasons Foundation, Bolia-
 nas, California – 325pp.)   1973
*The Gilgit Manuscript of the Astadasasahasrika Prajnapara-
 mita*, ch. 70 to 82, edited and translated (Serie
 Orientale Roma – 254pp.)   1974
The Short Prajnaparamita Texts (Luzac and Co., London
 – 217pp.)   1974
Further Buddhist Studies (B. Cassirer, Oxford – 238pp.)   1975
The Large Sutra on Perfect Wisdom (University of
 California Press – 679pp.)   1975

Divorced from his Buddhist studies and literary and translatory work was his professional career as a professor. From
1963 to 65, he was first the Distinguished Visiting Professor

of Indian Studies at the University of Wisconsin and then a Research Fellow at Manchester College, Oxford. For three years after '65, he had the distinction of being Professor of Indic Studies at the University of Washington, Seattle. Amongst his other prestigious responsibilities, was his Vice-Presidency of the Buddhist Society and the Custodian of Central Asian Manuscripts at the India Office Library, both in London. In 1968, he was first appointed a Visiting Professor of Comparative Religion at the University of Lancaster, an appointment which has been renewed until 1979. Between 1970 and 1973 he also went as a Visiting Professor of Buddhist Studies to the Friedrich Wilhelm Universitaet in Bonn and then to the University of California, first in Berkeley and then in Santa Barbara.

As if all that wasn't enough, Dr Conze has contributed something like 95 articles, 146 book reviews and 21 miscellaneous articles on Buddhist and non-Buddhist topics over the past thirty-five years to scores of journals and the like – and that was at the last count! And still, this brilliant man, the greatest living authority on the Mahayana in the West today, continues to translate, commentate and expound on the Buddhadharma.

As long as Dr Conze lives, we can be self-assured that here we have for the time being a master at his art. Here is a man who has used his own 'skilful means' to present to the West that 'wisdom which has gone beyond' so meticulously. His comprehension, if that be the right word, of the quintessence of the Prajnaparamita, namely, Sunyata or vast emptiness, is to be totally respected. When this light goes out, who, I wonder, will come forth and resume the scaling of the summitless mountain as Dr Conze has?

3 The Buddhist Society

1924–1967

The present Society, the oldest and most respected Buddhist organization in the West, has its roots in two precursors, the Buddhist Society of Great Britain and Ireland (established 1907) and the Buddhist Lodge (established 1924). The old Society was founded by Prof. T. W. Rhys Davids who took the office of President, Prof. E. T. Mills, FRS, as Chairman and Capt., J. E. Ellam as Hon. Secretary. At the Cavendish Rooms in Mortimer Street the founding meeting was held with the aim of proposing rules and regulations for controlling the Society's affairs. The objectives of the Society were the dissemination of basic Buddhist doctrines along with the systematic study of Pali, the language in which the words of the Buddha were first recorded. Some leading Buddhists of the time were Francis Payne, the leading Buddhist 'evangelist', Alexander Fisher, Dr Ernest Rost of the Indian Medical Service and the Hon. Eric Collier.

During this time a Londoner, Allan Bennett, had found himself enduring the long trip to Ceylon and later to Burma, where he was duly ordained into the Sangha. Upon taking the monastic name of Ananda Metteyya (he was ordained Maitreya but later changed it to the Pali equivalent), he set forth upon the project of leading a mission to England where he hoped to plant the seed of the Dhamma securely in Western soil. On 23 April 1907, the Mission from Burma arrived with

Ananda Metteyya announcing himself as the Secretary-General of the International Buddhist Society of Rangoon. After an immense magnitude of correspondence, interviews and lectures covering eight months, it was soon the Mission's time to leave.

A year later saw the launching of the first Buddhist periodical to appear in the West. This was *The Buddhist Review*, edited by J. E. Ellam. Among the formidable contributors were Prof. Rhys Davids, D. T. Suzuki, Mme David-Neel, Bhikkhu Silacara (J. F. McKechnie) and, of course, Ananda Metteyya. Buddhist books now extant included Dr Suzuki's *Outlines of Mahayana Buddhism*, *The Word of the Buddha* by Bhikkhu Silacara, the *Bodhicaryavatara* by Barnett and Rhys Davids's *Dialogues of the Buddha*.

During the four years of the war the Society's proceedings carried on, albeit with an air of despondency. Membership flagged, the *Review* was not published quite so often, and funds were hard to come by.

However, a post-war revival began in 1918 which saw new personalities arising and a new Editor of the *Review* in D. B. Jayatilaka. Ananda Metteyya was again in the forefront and a substantial sum of money was donated by Mr C. A. Hewivatarne and Anagarika Dharmapala of Ceylon to help the restoration of the Dhamma in England. The years of 1921 and 1922 saw the death of three remarkable figures in 'British Buddhism'; Prof. T. W. Rhys Davids, Prof. E. Mills and Frank Balls, who had held the post of General Secretary back in 1913. A year later Ananda Metteyya died at the age of fifty, which led to the emergence of Francis Payne to take over making known the Buddhadhamma in England. This took the form of twelve public lectures beginning in January 1923 and ending in May 1924. This helped to assuage the dissolution of the old Society and to contribute to the forming of a Buddhist Centre within the Theosophical Society which later became the Buddhist Lodge.

This new development was the work of a young and enthusiastic self-confessed Buddhist, Christmas Humphreys.

At seventeen years of age Christmas Humphreys discovered Buddhism from Coomaraswamy's *Buddha and the Gospel of Buddhism*. He later joined the Theosophical Society where he had the chance to develop his Buddhist studies in congenial surroundings. The effort and work put into his studies came to fruition with the founding of a Buddhist Centre within the Theosophical Society in June 1924. Later on that year the Centre joined resources with the Society to form the Buddhist Lodge, with Christmas Humphreys as President and Miss A. M. Faulkner (later Mrs Humphreys) as Hon. Secretary.

One of the vital functions provided by the new Lodge was a correspondence service carried out by A. C. March, primarily for isolated people and groups. Because of the increase in membership to the Lodge, a new magazine was conceived. This was the *Buddhist Lodge Monthly Bulletin*, first published in October 1925 and later (March 1926) renamed *Buddhism in England*.

In the same year a second Buddhist missionary arrived from the East. This was Anagarika Dharmapala from Ceylon, who could be termed a Buddhist Theosophist. Being a close associate of Mme H. P. Blavatsky, he renounced the householder life for that of a homeless wanderer* in search of Truth. In May of 1881 he founded the Mahabodhi Society of Calcutta, the earliest recorded Buddhist Society, and restored Buddha Gaya to Buddhist ownership once more. In 1925 he came to England and founded the British Mahabodhi Society. Hence, within two years there existed in London two Buddhist groups which, however, failed to amalgamate. Even to this day the British Mahabodhi Society claims to have laid the *spiritual* foundation stone of Buddhism in Britain.

During the remaining quarter of 1926 the Lodge was beginning to face dissolution. After an emergency meeting it was resolved to break away from the Theosophical Society, and after returning its Charter, it became an independent entity, adopting the name of The Buddhist Lodge, London. A special feature of the new Lodge was the publication of a text-book,

*The literal meaning of the term Anagarika.

What is Buddhism? After having appointed a committee whose work it was to analyse, criticize, approve or censure any of the scripts, drafts began to appear and within eighteen months the book was complete.

In May of 1927 Anagarika Dharmapala returned to England, invited by the British Mahabodhi Society and the Lodge, where in May one and all celebrated Wesak at the Essex Hall. Amongst some of the speakers were the Anagarika, Christmas Humphreys, Charles Galloway, and A. P. DeZoysa. Also in that year B. L. Broughton was elected President of the British Mahabodhi Society, Dr DeZoysa formed the Students Buddhist Association and Miss Aileen Faulkner married Christmas Humphreys.

The year 1928 proved fruitful with two main events supplying the talking points of that particular year. In October the much awaited text-book, *What is Buddhism? an Answer from the Western Point of View* was published. The toil and labour which constituted 256 pages of the book proved incredibly successful and to my knowledge ran into three editions. The other main event brought an unusual figure from China in the form of the Ven. Tai Hsu, the Abbot of Nan Pu To Monastery. This stocky, bespectacled Chinese proved a tower of strength in the revival of Chinese Buddhism, and apart from his other accomplishments, went down in Buddhist history as being the third Buddhist Mission to land on these shores..

The following year again saw a copious stream of publications, one of which gave a remarkable insight into that most secret of countries, Tibet, called *Intimate Glimpses of Mysterious Tibet*, by Dr McGovern. This book coincided with another of his books on Tibet called *To Lhasa in Disguise*. A. C. March, editor of *Buddhism in England* and now retired from full-time work, had published a popular text-book, *A Brief Glossary of Buddhist Terms*. Such was the availability of books on Buddhism, the Lodge's Library now consisted of some five hundred books.

In 1934 the first European Buddhist Congress was held at the British Mahabodhi Society. The main theme running through the speeches was the question, how can the Buddha-dhamma best improve itself in contemporary European society? Amongst the eminent Buddhists of the time at the Congress were Miss Constant Lounsberry, N. D. S. Silva, A. C. March, Daya Hewavitarne and the German Buddhist Ven. Tao Chun (Martin Steinke).

With meditation playing a major part in the Buddhist teaching, it still appeared that the practising Buddhists of the middle thirties were without a practical guide to meditative techniques. Hence the Lodge, after eighteen months' work published a handy and concise meditative manual, *Concentration and Meditation*. This was one of the first books of its kind to appear in British bookshops and adequately provided all the elemental practice and theory to develop meditative absorption. The Wesak festival of that year was held at Caxton Hall, the principal speakers being Mr Humphreys, Dr B. E. Fernando, Charles Galloway and a new member of the Lodge, Alan Watts. During this time A. C. March saw the publication of one of his most original books, *A Buddhist Bibliography*, which took him five years to compile. March, who had been suffering from eye trouble resigned from his post as Editor of the magazine, which Alan Watts took over. Alan Watts, whilst still only twenty-one, had written his understanding of Zen Buddhism in the form of *The Spirit of Zen*, which to me stands as one of the best expositions of Zen extant today. He later left for America in 1938 with his wife and Clare Cameron took over as Editor of the Journal.

The Second World War broke out in September of 1939 and brought with it, apart from untold suffering, a complete break of ties with various Buddhist Societies in Europe. Even in London all public meetings were temporarily halted. One of the burning questions which was asked of lay Buddhists of the time was – should a man forsake his country for the upholding of the principle of ahisma (non-injury) to fellow humans. Well, the Society's attitude was to honour each man for doing what he thought was ethically right.

The early years of the war brought acceptable change and

uncertainty which manifested in the change of headquarters from Mr and Mrs Humphreys's home in South Eaton Place to premises rented by the Lodge in Great Russell Street. A month later the Lodge was given a new name, The Buddhist Society. The fact that Buddhism was finding an ever expanding following amongst the English populace was evident by the increasing number of meetings held each week.

During 1945, Christmas Humphreys, whose study of the Dharma covered twenty years, was busy drafting a short document which would delineate the principles of Buddhism, both Theravada and Mahayana, yet still justify both schools' individual tenets. Thus, after the appropriate committee was formed and after hours of discussion and debate, 'Twelve Principles of Buddhism' were compiled, which are now recognized worldwide and have to date been published in sixteen languages. This was the setting for a tour of Buddhist countries throughout the world which Christmas Humphreys undertook, in the cause of representing the United Kingdom in Japan at the International Tribunal for the Far East, an ideal opportunity to savour the Buddhist centres of pilgrimage. His travels and experiences were, in 1948, reported in his book, *Via Tokyo*.

After the war a fresh spirit motivated the Society and various re-arrangements took place. Miss Joan Pope took up the post of General Secretary with Mr David Sherwood as Auditor. A Foreign Secretary was appointed, also an American Secretary, to document and enumerate the fast-increasing Buddhist communities in the States. Lastly, an Archivist, an essential need in the registration of historical and chronological data. Apart from pure historical facts, there also included various relics and works of art accumulated over the years.

In 1948 the then mysterious land of Tibet, which had for many centuries held the wonder and admiration of the West, disclosed some of its obscure culture by the presence of three Tibetan Buddhists who were visiting England on a trade mission. Headed by Tsepon Shakhaba, they presented the Society with various gifts along with the usual ceremonial white silk scarfs. On the whole, they were surprised at the apparent abundance of Tibetan Buddhist knowledge gleaned from the Society's members: much of which could be attributed to such early writers as Mme David-Neel and Dr McGovern.

A year later the Society celebrated its Silver Jubilee, twenty-five years of untiring effort, the *praemia virtutis* of the innovators of British Buddhism. Amongst the various celebrations which took place, there was an exhibition of Tibetan Art, and a meeting at Caxton Hall, the now-established centre for important meetings, where the Thai Ambassador to Britain presented a magnificent Shrine to the Society. Mr Christmas Humphreys with the generous consideration of Mr A. S. Frere of Heinemann's had his *Zen Buddhism* published to coincide with the Society's Jubilee.

Twenty-five years is a comparatively long time in the formation of any new organization, but looked at in the light of a new religion, and an Eastern one at that, which proclaims a doctrine largely antithetical to that of Christianity, it would seem that Buddhism was firmly established and had taken root in yet another Christian country. The growth, by now characteristic of this ecumenical religion, was by no means limited to London and the home counties. By 1952 there were flourishing Buddhist groups, who were all affiliated to the Buddhist Society in Manchester, Edinburgh, Oxford, Cambridge and Brighton, which Mr Humphreys has pointed out as being a result, to a certain extent, of the popularity of his small Pelican paperback, *Buddhism*, which appropriately was published in 1951 on his fiftieth birthday.

If there is one fact of existence which characterizes our every plan and system, it is that of impermanence. The Society's premises at Great Russell Street met the inevitable winds of change in June of 1952, when the lease came to an end. However, within three months an offer was made by London University's China Committee to re-house the Society at 16 Gordon Square. At the official opening there appeared a distinguished guest list which included the Ambassadors of

Japan and Thailand and the High Commissioners of India and Ceylon.

Mrs A. A. G. Bennett, who had briefly succeeded Clare Cameron as Editor, resigned in the summer of 1952 and handed over this important post to Mrs M. H. Robins. *The Middle Way* by now the most important Buddhist magazine in the West, was given great help by a generous gift from Thailand, which enabled the Society to enlarge its size and circulation.

The most respected authority on Zen Buddhism, Dr D. T. Suzuki, was a welcomed visitor to the Society in the summer of 1953 where he gave lectures and instruction on Zen practice. The mere presence of this great scholar gave to the Zen class much encouragement. Dr Suzuki also addressed the Summer School of that year alongside other speakers as Dr Edward Conze, Mr Maurice Walshe, Miss I. B. Horner and the Samanera Dhammananda.

The Wesak celebrations of 1954 included amongst other things the publication of Dr Conze's much-overdue *Buddhist Texts*. Dr Conze was aided in his work by three other eminent scholars in Miss I. B. Horner, Dr Snellgrove and Dr Waley.

By October 1956, the Society moved to its present headquarters at 58 Eccleston Square, SW1. The move to the new headquarters coincided with the Buddha Jayanti, the celebration of the 2500th anniversary of the Buddha's Enlightenment, which began with a meeting of representatives from various Buddhist countries at Ceylon House. Amongst other celebrations in London there took place a Buddhist Film Show, an over-crowded Wesak meeting at Caxton Hall, the usual Summer School, which seemed to attract a larger than usual throng of meditators and a delegation was sent to the 7th Conference of the World Fellowship of Buddhists in New Delhi.

Tibet was invaded in 1959 by the Chinese Communists whereupon the Dalai Lama along with 25,000 other Tibetans fled to India. It is because of this historic calamity that we in the West now enjoy a knowledge of Tibetan Buddhism unparalleled in world thought. In London, this occasioned the setting up of The Tibet Society, which was given accommodation at the Buddhist Society. A year later saw the publication of a treatise on Tibetan Buddhism by the German-born Anagarika Govinda, called *Foundations of Tibetan Mysticism*. Here was a dissertation on the mystical mantra, 'Om Mani Padma Hum', never before attempted by a Western author. From this time on Lama Govinda proved that he was one of the leading non-Tibetan authorities on the 'Adamantine Path'. One of the Tibetan Lamas who came to the West with the intention of setting up a Tibetan Centre was the Lama Chogyam Trungpa Rimpoche, well known for his excellent book, *Born in Tibet*.*

In 1964 the publication of two important books directly associated with the Society furnished its bookstall. Firstly, Christmas Humphreys had his *Buddhism* published, a text-book covering the fundamentals of Buddhist doctrine. Secondly, a booklet entitled *100 Treasures of the Buddhist Society*, a roster of different ornaments, books, etc., accumulated over the years. The return of the Ven. Sangharakshita from his twenty years' 'exile' in India also took place in this memorable year.

On 12 July, 1966, the great Japanese Zen Buddhist scholar and writer, Dr Daisetz Teitaro Suzuki passed away at the age of ninety-five. His death was a loss, not only to the East but to the West, as most of his life-long literary effort was devoted to the enlightenment of the 'Zen Mind' in Europe and America. He was a personal friend of the Buddhist Society and in particular the Society's Zen class which he had instructed on many occasions. As a personal caprice, I will always remember Suzuki for his three volumes, *Essays in Zen Buddhism*, which for me were his greatest works, unequalled in Zen literature, both East and West.

Just over a year later another great loss was sustained by the Society; this time it was one of the Co-Founders of the Society, Arthur C. March (1880–1967). A brilliant Buddhist scholar, he was the founder of *The Buddhist Lodge Monthly*

*Lama Trungpa Rimpoche along with Lama Akong Tarap Rimpoche were directly responsible for the founding of Samye-Ling Tibetan Centre in 1967. See Chapter 5, page 106.

Bulletin, the early precursor of the *Middle Way*, which he edited for ten years. He wrote such books as *A Brief Glossary of Buddhist Terms, an Analysis of the Pali Canon*, and is renowned for his voluminous work, *A Buddhist Bibliography*.

On 25 November, 1967 the Society had occasion to celebrate the Diamond Jubilee of Buddhism in England. This was held at Eccleston Square, presided over by Christmas Humphreys who outlined the requirements for more leaders and writers to carry on the propagation of the Dharma in the West. During the autumn of that same year the Society welcomed from the Ryutakuji Temple in Japan the Ven. Sotchu Suzuki, a noteworthy Rinzai Roshi. Throughout the autumn he conducted meditation classes in the tradition of Rinzai Zen.

The last ten years

Buddha Day (Wesak), was celebrated in May of 1968 at Dennison House. Amongst the distinguished visitors at the occasion were Sir Lalita Rajapakse (High Commissioner of Ceylon), the Nepalese Ambassador and Madame Misra and HRH the Ambassador for Laos and Princess Khammas.

Pansil was led by the Ven. Chao Khun Sobhana Dhammasuddhi, followed by a lecture from him on the Buddha's Enlightenment. Other speakers during the course of the proceedings were Miss Diana Moore and Mrs M. H. Robins.

The President's Report for that year showed a sharp rise in subscriptions to the *Middle Way*, a sure sign that more and more people were being attracted to Buddhism. During that year the Lama Trungpa Rimpoche ran a series of monthly lectures on Saturdays and Sundays on Tibetan Buddhism. Also at the Society the well known Japanese Zen Master, Ven. Sochu Suzuki ran a popular Zen meditation class on Friday evenings.

The Fourth Buddhist Conference was held at the Society's headquarters where representatives travelled from Aberdeen, Brighton, Cambridge, Colchester, Devon, Doncaster, Sussex, Glasgow, Hull, and Leicester to name but a few, again another indication of how popular Buddhism was becoming in Britain.

During this year two of England's most famous present-day Buddhists had published books which outlined in diverse ways their involvement with Buddhism over the years. These were Christmas Humphreys's *Sixty Years of Buddhism in England* and Dr Edward Conze's *Thirty Years of Buddhist Studies*.

The Buddha Day celebrations of 1969 came back again to Caxton Hall, the main speakers being Christmas Humphreys (Chairman), Phirotz Mehta and Dr Karol Werner. Anne Lobstein (now Anne Bancroft) and Carlo Robins gave readings from the scriptures. The Ven. Phra Maha Boonchuay brought the proceedings to a close by leading the audience in chanting the Suttas. Two distinctive books published that year were Chogyam Trungpa's *Meditation in Action* and Alan Watts's *The Book*.

During this year the Society reported a 100 per cent rise in book sales. By now the lay or prospective Buddhist had an array of Buddhist publications from which to choose. Alan Watts visited the Society and brought with him a prized possession, a colour film on Tibetan Buddhism which was aptly entitled 'Requiem for a Faith'. Two other distinguished visitors to the Society were Dr Klar, the Secretary of the Buddhist Federation of Germany and Mr Sanam Topgay, the interpreter to HH the Dalai Lama.

By 1970, the steady progress in book sales became strikingly evident, enhanced by the fact that elections to membership were running at approximately twenty per month. At the Group Conference the Society assembled members of the Theravada, Tibetan and Japanese Sanghas for the first time, which added an authentic touch to the proceedings. The Correspondence Course, the only one of its kind dealing with basic Buddhism in the country, was requested to be published abroad. A definite sign of the popularity of a course explaining in a simple, yet scholarly way, the doctrines of Buddhism.

This year, the Society attempted what I can only describe as a brave gesture to the ever growing contingency of Buddhists, not only in Britain, but in the Western world. This was a 10-inch high plaster Buddha image created by the sculptor

Mr Cubitt Bevis, showing the countenance not of an Oriental but of a Western man. To stare at this piece instilled in one an uncanny incredulity that I felt was just a little bit out of place. We are conditioned by cultural developments and traits of a country's history, but this image tended to undermine the image we all have of the Buddharupa. However, the actual figure was beautifully and thoughtfully sculptured by a man renowned for his portrayal of Thomas O'Beckett.

There were several outstanding books published this year but I feel that John Blofeld's *The Way of Power*, a must for all those interested in the theory and practice of Tantric Buddhism, *Zen Mind, Beginners Mind* by Shunryu Suzuki and D. T. Suzuki's *The Training of the Zen Buddhist Monk* came top of the list.

On 27 August, a retinue of twenty-eight priests and laymen from Japan visited the Society. They were members of the Japan Buddhist Cultural Association led by the Most Reverend Sinzen Koike, the Archbishop of the Suma Buddhist Temple, Kobe.

During May of 1971, the Conference of Buddhist Groups got under way. The main delegates to the Conference were the Ven. Somboon Siddiyana (Buddhapadipa Wat), Ven. Shanti Bhadra Thera (London Buddhist Vihara), Akong Tarap Rimpoche and the Ven. Lama Chime Rimpoche. Mr Humphreys outlined the Society's plans to help associated groups by cutting prices by 25 per cent on books and the taped lecture-hiring scheme. He also stressed, with a word of warning, that it is all too easy to be side-tracked into comparing, analysing and integrating Buddhist doctrines with other philosophies. After tea a formal discussion on World Buddhism in general, and on Europe in particular, ensued. An incidental feature of the headquarters was that the building was included in a roster of historical places of interest.

On 8 October, the Society lost a sincere and devoted Buddhist in Mrs Ruth Walshe. She worked hard for the Society during the years and was always willing to lecture when the need arose. She will be remembered for the energy she exercised in the running of the main meditation class. In the form of a *memoria technica*, a Japanese image was reposited in the Lecture Hall.

In 1971 a profusion of Buddhist books appeared on the bookshelves which included *Buddhist Poems* by Christmas Humphreys, *A Primer of Soto Zen* by Masunaga, *Treasures on the Tibetan Middle Way* by Herbert Guenther, *The Buddha's Way* by Ven. Saddhatissa, *Buddhism and Death* by M. Walshe and *The Way of Chuang Tzu* by Father Merton.

Buddha Day took place on 1 May 1972 at Caxton Hall. As usual Pansil was taken by everyone, this time being conducted by the Ven. Chao Khun Phra Medhidhammacarya, the then Senior Incumbent of the Buddhapadipa Wat Temple.

His Eminence the High Commissioner for India, Mr Aba B. Pant, spoke at length for the ever growing need to realize that deepest wisdom or 'that which is within'. He expressed his feeling that the West's desire for technological advancement was symptomatic of their 'lust after illusory power'. The evening came to an end with the now 'traditional' chanting, led this time in Tibetan by the Ven. Lama Chime Rimpoche, followed by meditation.

New publications included *Buddhist Meditation* by Dr Conze, *Mudra* by Chogyam Trungpa Rimpoche and *Living by Zen*, by Dr Suzuki.

A steady feature and now not so unusual was the growing book sales and the increase of membership – not only confined to Britain, I might add. The Correspondence Course figured largely in the proceedings of this year and a total revision of the subject matter was carried out by the skilful expertise of Maurice Walshe, Burt Taylor and the Course Director, Arthur Blundell.

In June of 1973 the Society had a great and honourable pleasure to welcome HH the Sakay Trizin, Head of the Sakya Order of Tibetan Buddhism. He stopped off in Britain for a week en route to Canada. His Holiness was welcomed at the Society by Christmas Humphreys, Sir Olaf Caroe (President of The Tibet Society) and Lama Chime Rimpoche. After speeches by Chime Rimpoche and Mr Humphreys, His Holiness wasted no time in expressing the point that the cultivation of compassion and kindness was a prerequisite towards developing Bodhicitta for the benefit and Enlightenment of all living beings. He also expressed his deepest thanks to the Tibet Society for the assistance given over the years.

Zen and Tibetan publications dominated the bookshelves and book reviews of the year, especially *The Secret and the Sublime* by John Blofeld, *The Art of Tantra* by P. Rawson, *The Zen Life* by Kaji Sato and *Unsui, A Diary of Zen Monastic Life* by E. Nishimura.

A year later two striking events captured the imagination, both of consummate importance. Firstly, there was the Dalai Lama's visit,* a momentous occasion in British Buddhism, and, secondly, the Society's Golden Jubilee.

On 16 November 1974 the Founder President, Mr Christmas Humphreys, welcomed to the headquarters at Eccleston Square for its Fiftieth Anniversary, many of those people who over the years have contributed to the advancement of the Buddhadharma as presented through the Buddhist Society. Some notables were Mr Phiroz Metha, U Kyaw Min and Tha Thun Aung from Burma, Prof. Ryotatsu Shioiri from Japan, Dr Walpola Rahula, Miss Horner from the Pali Text Society, Miss Joan Pope, General Secretary of the Society for nineteen years, Mrs Carlo Robins, Editor and Tom Harris, Chairman of the Summer School. The Celebration and Reception held at Caxton Hall five days later was attended by an unusually large audience.

Christmas Humphreys commenced the proceedings by asserting how rare it was to find himself still remaining President after half a century – an exceptional achievement. He spoke at length of the war years, those bitter years when not only the Society's future was in jeopardy, but the democratic and free society, the only kind of society where spiritual and high moral standards are tantamount to peace and understanding. Other speakers during the day were the Ven. Saddhatissa, Mr

*See pages 151–9.

Alf Vial, now studying Tibetan texts in India and Burt Taylor. Lama Chime Rimpoche brought the proceedings to a close by chanting, in Tibetan, blessings to all those in attendance.

Another individual event which took place in this memorable year was the publication of a special Jubilee edition of the *Middle Way*, including a brief history of the Society written by Christmas Humphreys.

Suddenly, in 1975, Mrs Christmas Humphreys died. As a Co-Founder of the Society, she served as a constant critic and consultant of her husband's work and was herself, a devout Buddhist. In 1927 she married Christmas Humphreys in a 'Buddhist Marriage' service conceived by them both. Like her husband, she was a sincere practitioner of Zen, and as far as I can gather, drew inspiration and guidance from her 'nigh worn' copy of Blyth's *Mumonkan*. After a private cremation service, there was held at the Society's headquarters, a Memorial Service attended by many friends, relations and members.

The main developments in 1976 revolved around the Correspondence Course. Firstly, at a council meeting, it was decided to begin a liaison service between affiliated groups throughout Britain. This was effected by appointing a Central Liaison Officer, Mr Nigel Watkins, who was the Correspondence Course Director. Under him were a number of Local Liaison Officers who, it was hoped, would be ideally group secretaries. The work of the LLOs would be to correspond or meet with isolated Buddhists in their own 'constituency', where personal or Dharma problems could be hopefully solved. Being closely linked to the Buddhist Society, it was hoped that these people along with the Central Liaison Officer, will be able, in the future, to provide a more personal service through a more integrated network of people and groups in the Dharma. Some ideas have already been discussed to achieve the above aim, mainly the publication of an inter-group newsletter, taped questions from groups on recorded lectures which are on sale at the Society, joint meetings and visiting speakers.

The other main development was a follow-up to the present Correspondence Course. I think the feeling has been that those who have successfully completed the course have experienced a void and that a continuing advanced course would be an ideal way of advancing in Buddhist studies and delving ever deeper into the inexhaustible Dharma. This would be manipulated by basing the course on existing texts, with each student being attached to tutors who would advise, assist and correct any mistakes in the students' work.

In May, a fiftieth Anniversary edition of the *Middle Way* was published which had many articles by leading Buddhist writers, alongside several authentic pictures of Mr Humphreys, etc. Christmas Humphreys also contributed his own 'picture' of the Buddhist Society over the past fifty years.

Amongst an ever growing profusion of Buddhist publications, I feel the following were the most significant:

The Thousand Petalled Lotus – Ven. Sangharakshita
Thomas Merton on Zen – compiled by Irmgard Schloegl
Kindly Bent to Ease Us – Herbert V. Guenther
Zen Master Dogen – Yuho Yokoi
Creative Meditation and Multi Dimensional Consciousness –
   Lama Anagarika Govinda

And so we come to 1977, a year which saw the return of the Gyalwa Karmapa to Britain. It would be foolish to try to envisage what developments will take place over the next fifty years. One thing is for certain, and that is throughout the past ten years the Society has seen a growth of membership, both within Britain and abroad, and that if this continues the Society, I am sure, will reciprocate by continuing its ideal service to the lay Buddhists of Britain. And I would personally hope that in the future the Society can find such a praiseworthy President as Christmas Humphreys, whom even in his seventy-seventh year is still as active a Buddhist as he ever was, then I hold the view of a secure and prosperous future ahead.

4   Flowers of Wisdom – the Theravada Tradition

As upon a heap of rubbish thrown on the highway, a sweet smelling, lovely lotus there may grow, even so amongst the rubbish of beings, a disciple of the Fully Enlightened One outshines the blind worldlings with wisdom.*

THE DHAMMAPADA
vs. 58 and 59.

The London Buddhist Vihara and the British Mahabodhi Society

These two institutions have had a coeval existence for many years now and both have to thank the diligence of the late Anagarika Dharmapala for their presence on the British Buddhist scene. Although the British Mahabodhi Society came first, it has now become apparent that if the Vihara closed then the British Mahabodhi Society would come to an end. However, in its twenty-three year history, the Vihara has never looked in jeopardy and the BMS is as strong today as it has ever been.

Anagarika Dharmapala came to Britain from Ceylon in the late 1890s, a guest of none other than Sir Edwin Arnold. He stayed in Britain surveying the spiritual and intellectual atmosphere of the people and returned to Ceylon two months

*Narada Thera's translation published in 'The Wisdom of the East' series by John Murray, 1954, p. 27.

C

later. It was obvious from Dharmapala's first visit to Britain that he was much encouraged and heartened at what he saw and that a return was imminent in the near future. But his second visit only materialized in 1925 where his work concentrated on establishing a 'Buddhist Mission' to be used as a centre for disseminating the Theravada doctrine.

A year later (1926) he managed to buy a house at 86 Madeley Road, Ealing, which he named Foster House, after Mary Foster of Hawaii, who donated thousands of dollars to Dharmapala in aid of his project. The BMS was officially inaugurated on Dhammacahka Day, 24 July but still remained under the title of 'The Buddhist Mission'. Amongst the speakers on that memorable occasion were Mr Christmas Humphreys, Anagarika Dharmapala, Francis J. Payne and Arthur C. March. But the Society's top priority was and still is the supporting, both financially and morally, of the Vihara.

Two years later, in February, 1928, the Anagarika had collected enough money to buy a property, the site in question being at 41 Gloucester Road, Regent's Park. Dharmapala's intention, although he was controlling operations back in Ceylon, was to found a Western branch of the Theravadin Sangha, an innovatory ideal at that time. Within five months, Dharmapala had sent the first three bhikkhus to take up residence in London. The three being Vens. H. Nandasara, D. Pannasara and P. Vajiranana* whose first tasks were to master the English language and to study Western culture. They were brought to Britain under the care of Devapriya Walisinha, the General Secretary of the parent Mahabodhi Society.

Activities at the Vihara were conducted by resident bhikkhus and took the form of a popular Sunday lecture around 5.00 or 6.00 o'clock. Periodically a visiting speaker would address the class on a topical subject and, in both cases, would be followed by a question-and-answer period. Added to this was a class in Pali and a meditation period in the Shrine Room.

---

*Ven. P. Vajiranana was probably the most distinguished resident at the Vihara (1928–32) by virtue of being the first bhikkhu to obtain a doctorate at Cambridge in 1936.

The Vihara provided a sanctuary for those Buddhists, both Asian and English, who were committed to the Theravada path and provided a focal point for Dhamma studies. It also contained a library which housed volumes of the Pali Canon along with other original ola-leaf manuscripts.

By 1930 the Vens. H. Nandasara and D. Pannasara returned to Ceylon, leaving Ven. P. Vajiranana to run the affairs of the Vihara, but in July, 1932 two Indian bhikkhus arrived in England to take up residence. They were Ven. Rahula Sankrityayana, who stayed for two years, and Ven. Ananda Kausalyayana, who also stayed for two years and who is still alive and living in India. The incumbency of the Vihara changed hands regularly and up until the outbreak of war was held by a Sinhalese bhikkhu, Ven. R. Siddhartha, from 1933 to 37 and Ven. D. Pannasara (mentioned earlier) from 1938 to 40, when the Vihara officially closed.

The whole Buddhist world was shocked, when in 1933, the news appeared of the death of Anagarika Dharmapala. A stalwart missionary, Dharmapala who, although he only enjoyed two years as a fully ordained bhikkhu, was the first to be ordained in India for seven hundred years. He will probably be remembered most for his missionary work as a 'homeless wanderer' expounding the Dhamma and for his untiring effort in returning Buddha Gaya to the Buddhists.

As mentioned elsewhere, the Vihara closed in 1940 and did not reopen until 1954. During those years the most hopeful and interesting project was the idea of a Buddhist Vihara Society, whose main target was the creation of a Vihara and ostensibly a Theravadin Sangha. This idea was furthered by five Sinhalese philanthropists headed by Sir Cyril de Zoysa.* After the formation of a Trust to re-establish the Vihara, the above mentioned managed to buy a lease on the property at 10 Ovington Gardens, S W 3, which forthwith was opened on Vesakha Day, 1954.

After the unfurling of the Buddhist flag by the Thai Ambassador, the proceedings continued with a plethora of speeches

*Currently the President of the Mahabodhi Society of Ceylon.

from Ven. Narada Mahathera, Miss Constant Lounsbery
of Les Amis du Bouddhisme Paris, Lt-Col. Payne (the son of
Francis Payne who died earlier in the year), U Maung Maung
Ji (Press Attaché of the Burmese Embassy) and Mr Christmas
Humphreys, President of The Buddhist Society. One felt at this
time that the reality of a Theravada Sangha based inLond on
was one giant step forward for more British Buddhists to join
their Oriental brothers 'in the robe', and hopefully, an expansion of the Sangha in any of its interdenominational forms.

With Ven. Narada as Incumbent along with Ven. Vinita,
the Vihara began a programme of expansion unequalled before
the war. Activities were more numerous with mid-week
classes alongside the Sunday lecture. An admired speaker of
the day was G. F. Allen who had undergone a year in the Order
in Ceylon and had now returned to found the Buddha Study
Association.* This group had its being within the precincts of
the Vihara and held classes in Buddhist doctrine, specializing in
Abhidhamma studies.

Vens. Narada and Vinita were replaced in 1955-6 by Vens.
Mirisse Gunasiri and K. Mahanama, during which preparations
were under way for the Buddha Jayanti Year (1956). During
the celebrations, which were universal throughout the Buddhist
world, there subsisted two public meetings. One was held at
Ovington Gardens, Knightsbridge, the other at Conway Hall,
Holborn, in conjunction with the Buddhist Society. During
this eventful year, Dr Dora Fonseka had published a *Jayanti
Number* (a collection of seven essays related to Buddhadhamma
practice) for the London Buddhist Association (which helped
to maintain the Vihara).

In April 1957, a new Incumbent took over the Vihara; he
was the Ven. Dr H. Saddhatissa, a learned Sinhalese bhikkhu
of many years' standing. For all those who know him, I'm
sure they will agree with me in saying that he is probably the
most revered and learned figure in 'Western' Theravadin
Buddhism today.

Ven. Saddhatissa was born into a relatively well-off family,

*G. F. Allen wrote *The Buddha's Philosophy*, published in 1958.

considering the standard of life in Ceylon at that time. Even from an early age he always had the aspiration to become a monk, and to lead a life exemplifying that of the Buddha Gotama's. This burning desire for the spiritual life came to a head when he left home, whilst still a youngster, and joined the Order in 1926. After his initial training in Ceylon and Burma, he spent eighteen years in India at Banaras Hindu University, where he taught Pali, Sanskrit and Buddhist doctrine. Apart from four short books printed in Sinhala, he helped to edit the *Pali Tipitakam Concordance*. Another selfless feature of this bhikkhu was the work he did with the 'untouchables' in Indian society.

From 1966 to 1969 he held the distinguished post of first Professor of Buddhism at Toronto University in Canada and popularized Pali and Theravada studies in that city. His industrious attitude in presenting Buddhism to the West blossomed in a spate of books on basic Buddhism which comprised: *The Upasakajanalankara*, ed. 1965, PTS, London (this had been his PhD thesis at Edinburgh University in 1963); *Buddhist Ethics* (1970), *The Buddha's Way* (1971) and *The Life of the Buddha* (1976) all printed by George Allen and Unwin, London. Another, more specialized but still significant contribution to Pali and Buddhist studies was his *Dasabodhisattuppattikatha* and the *Birth Stories of the Ten Bodhisattas* (PTS, 1975). Ven. Saddhatissa, to me, explains Buddhism in a simple, dignified and encouraging way. His faith and erudition in the Dhamma is like his gentle demeanour, ineffably egregious. In my brief acquaintance with him I found a man who, although not in the best of health, showed compassion and kindness; an emanation having at its centre a brilliant multi-faceted diamond shedding light unveiled by samsaric confusion.

Ven. Saddhatissa is currently still the Head of the Vihara and has seen many bhikkhus come and go in the past twenty years, notably: Vens. Vinita (resident in 1964), H. Dhammaloka, Sumanashanta, K. Mahanama (not to be confused with Ven. Gunasiri's colleague) and Ven. M. Vajiranana (now i/c British Buddhist Association). At the present, apart from

Ven. Dr Saddhatissa, the Vens. K. Piyatissa and H. Khemananda are resident at the Vihara.

In 1960, an up-and-coming Londoner called Russell Webb became associated with the Vihara and eventually, through hard work I may add, became Hon. Secretary in 1964 of the British Mahabodhi Society and joint editor of its journal, *Buddhist Quarterly* in 1968. He has related to me how, whilst in the last year of school, he began to have doubts about Christianity. Although still a member of a congregational church, he set about studying comparative religion, and met a lay Buddhist who consequently introduced him to the London Vihara.

Russell literally educated himself, most of his reading material coming from the Buddhist Publication Society, Kandy. In fact the first book he read was Narada's *Buddhism in a Nutshell* which he termed a 'perennial classic'. He studied 'religiously' Theravada doctrine as a basis for the rest of Buddhist training. Russell only loosely associated with the Vihara at first. However, through time it was obvious that here he had found something so precious and inviting that a vocational 'career' with the Vihara became a major attraction. His first major task was to catalogue the hundreds of texts and literature which had grown through the years, a task he dearly loved. He then became, as mentioned earlier, the Secretary of the BMS and joint editor of its journal – two very responsible and taxing posts.

In 1963 the original trustees acquired a freehold property at Chiswick whereupon the management of the Vihara was taken over by the Mahabodhi Society of Ceylon. Its Secretary Lalit Hewavitarne, a member of Dharmapala's family, came over to London and personally picked the site at Chiswick, which was not too far removed from central London and was amply served by bus and tube. The move was decided in the winter of 1963 and by the following spring the transfer was effected from Ovington Gardens with bhikkhus moving in almost immediately.

The Grand Opening of the new Vihara was held at Vesahka,

attended by Miss I. B. Horner (President of the Pali Text Society), Mr Christmas Humphreys, the Mayor of Chiswick and many other personalities and a public procession was held, with much pomp and spectacle. To mark the first official entry into Britain of a relic of the Buddha, a procession was held in October of that year. It wound round Turnham Green, led by Russell Webb holding aloft the Buddhist flag, followed by two elephants from Billy Smart's Circus. As one can well nigh imagine, this march was well covered in the media, which was a shrewd method of gaining publicity for the new Buddhist centre. The whole proceedings were considerably enhanced by the appearance and participation of Earl Mountbatten, the Bishop of London and others, whilst the whole 'show' was brilliantly stage-managed by the High Commissioner for Ceylon, Dr G. P. Malalasekera. The latter was a devout Buddhist and became a patron of the Vihara. The procession was preceded by a public meeting in the Town Hall where church dignitaries and diplomats met and talked about their respective beliefs.

The Vihara was acquired due largely to the persistence and toil of Ven. Saddhatissa. The relic of the Buddha, a splinter of bone, was encased in a glass receptacle, mounted on an ornate brass pedestal and retained in a brass canopy – all of which was enshrined in the Shrine Room. This makes the Vihara 'sacred ground', as tradition has it that a Vihara or Shrine Room which houses relics of the Buddha is considered blessed and holy.

The British Mahabodhi Society, originally founded by Dharmapala in 1926, was revived in 1966 by Ven. Saddhatissa. The aims of the Society are still unchanged, in other words, to provide support for the maintenance of the Vihara, which it administers in its capacity as a registered charity.

During the last ten years or so, as with other Buddhist groups and societies, it has been a matter of self-preservation and expansion with ever new motives coming into play in making widespread the teachings of the Buddha. However, a recent development of the Society has been its Graduated

Reading Course which has superseded the Correspondence
Course, originally written and conceived by Mr A. Haviland-
Nye (Hon. Treasurer for many years and now joint head of the
British Buddhist Association). The Reading Course takes on
the form of the study often *Wheel* booklets (from the BPS,
Kandy) which introduces basic Buddhism to the beginner in a
simple and uncomplicated way. These are sent out at monthly
intervals covering the three sections of the Eightfold Path,
namely, sila, samadhi and panna.* The course terminates with
the presentation of Ven. Nyanatiloka's classic anthology,
The Word of the Buddha.

In its fifty-one years' history, the London Vihara and/or the
British Mahabodhi Society has provided various journals for
the lay Buddhist, which began way back in 1926 with *The
British Buddhist*, the brainchild of Dharmapala himself. This
bulletin, which was published monthly, began with eight pages
and, because of its demand, expanded into a magazine. It
terminated in 1934.

In 1935, the journal, for various reasons changed format and
became a cyclosyled bulletin called *The Wheel* (with no
connections whatsoever with the present *Wheel* publications
of the BPS, Kandy). It ran from 1935 to 1939 and was
published monthly. During the war years and up until 1964
no journal was published.

In 1968, under the joint editorship of Ven. Saddhatissa and
Mr Russell Webb, *Buddhist Quarterly* was launched, succeeding
the previous monthly bulletin called *Buddhist News* (1964–8),
a two-page spread. *Buddhist Quarterly*, as it exists today, is a
thirty to forty page journal which incorporates a sutta-
translation by Ven. Saddhatissa, two or three articles dealing
with Dhamma studies, news and notes, mainly on Buddhist
centres in the West and a book review, a must for all scholarly
journals. Throughout, one finds snippets of Anagarika Dharmapala's 'words of wisdom', one of which appears at the end of
this section.

The Vihara, at 5 Heathfield Gardens, Chiswick, has a
*i.e., morality, concentration and wisdom.

capacious Lecture Hall where meetings and lectures are conducted. This hall also contains within it, the library, an authentic array of Pali texts, ola-leaf manuscripts, various journals, 'comparative' Buddhist works, etc., all of which add up to an impressive 2000-volume collection. Allied to this is the Vihara's book stall which, because of its close connections with BPS, Kandy,* sells most of the former's publications. As most readers will know, the BPS is a society dealing in the main with Theravada literature. Their *Wheel* and *Bodhi Leaves* series are probably the most widely known and respected examples of Theravadin Buddhist literature, with the *Wheel* publications amounting to an incredible 236 issues and *Bodhi Leaves* having 73 in its 'A' and 'B' series. Apart from these, there are many other books on sale dealing with Theravada Buddhism from a variety of widely divergent authors.

In 1975, a purpose-built meditation hall was built at the rear of the Vihara. Here, the layman can retire either privately but, more often, in a group for meditation. The hall which contains a beautifully pure white Buddha, illuminated by a 'hidden' light gives one a sense of beatitude fitting for one about to partake in inner peace.

Activities and Retreats

Sundays are busy days at the Vihara with hour-long Dhamma lessons for children commencing at 10.00 a.m. In the latter part of the afternoon, a beginner's class in Buddhism is held at 4.00 p.m., with devotions and meditation at 5.00. This meditation comprises a half an hour's practice of anapanasati or mindfulness of breathing. There are also held in the same session a ten-minute recitation of the scriptures conducted by a resident bhikkhu. A lecture sermon commences at 6.00 p.m.

On Wednesdays, you are invited to join a class in the Pali language at 6.00 p.m., followed by a meditation class which begins at 7.30 p.m. and ends at 9.00.

*For more information contact: London Buddhist Vihara or, direct to Buddhist Publication Society, P O Box 61, Kandy, Sri Lanka.

A quarterly meditation retreat is also held at the Vihara where the primary practice is intensive all-day meditations, held on the first Saturdays in March, June, September and December. Each session commences at 9.30 a.m. and lunch is provided for the participants. As this is a meditation retreat, reading and other distracting activities are advised against.

I hope you find your visit both worthwhile and enlightening as I did.

Those who wish to get at Truth, should not be contented with the myths and theories of the mystics and ascetics. They should be daring, courageous and full of intense earnestness.

ANAGARIKA DHARMAPALA*

The Buddhist Centre, Oaken Holt

Oaken Holt is a magnificent Victorian country mansion lying a couple of miles from the city of Oxford, close to the village of Farmoor. I had the good fortune to visit the Buddhist Centre back in 1973, having the basic finances and elementary commodities of sleeping-bag, shaving kit, toothbrush, pen and notebook and last, but certainly not least, a translation of the *Dhammapada*. As the rules at that time decreed, one supplied one's own food and no heating facilities in the way of a primus stove was supplied – such was the strictness of the Centre; an austere rule perhaps! But if you knew Mr Saw, the owner and, incidentally, a pious Burmese Buddhist, you would soon learn that strict meditation was *the* order of the day, not a frolicking avocation in the orchards and woods which surround the house. If you came to meditate – then just meditate – nothing else.

The mansion, which was owned and built by the late Sir William Hunter after his retiral from the Indian Civil Service in 1875, stands on approximately forty acres of some of England's most beautiful countryside. Sir William was the Head of the Indian Educational Service and was a keen writer. Although he was an educationalist, most of his works concentrated on Indian history. He was in the mould of the upper-class pristine Victorian gentry. His biography, which is 'housed' at Oaken Holt, is an excellent example of the puritanical 'caste' of the day.

Much later the mansion was sold to Lord Abingdon and became the family seat of Lord Abingdon for thirty years.

After such notable and highly esteemed inhabitants, Oaken Holt fell into the hands of the National Provincial Bank, and was used as a Training Centre for junior staff. This lasted for some twenty-five years. The residential trainees were housed in the rectangular wooden bungalows to the rear of the house. Each bungalow, divided into eighteen cubicles or 'box rooms', provided accommodation for ninety people and, which today, serves the purpose of accommodating short- and long-term meditators to the Centre.

In 1969, the National Provincial and Westminster Banks amalgamated becoming the National Westminster Bank. Because of this merger, Oaken Holt was put up for sale early in 1972.

During this time, a Burmese businessman called U Myat Saw, who had lived in Britain for several years, had the wish to found a Buddhist centre. This would ideally be a centre of retreat dealing and providing for strict meditators under simple surroundings. Mr Saw looked around much of the south of England for the ideal property, even possibly a hotel. The ideal was for a hotel to finance the Buddhist Centre out of its own profits. Food, bedding, and conveniences would already be provided whereas all the profits of the Centre could then be used to finance visiting speakers, courses and seminars, etc. Mr Saw looked at various out-of-the-way country hotels in Surrey, Sussex, Hampshire and, finally, Oxfordshire.

However, this ideal, it transpired, created many ethical problems, namely, the selling of alcohol and various other 'unwholesome' contrivances not in favour with Buddhist morality. The upkeep of a Buddhist community by profits from the above-mentioned activities would be a total contradiction in principles. Thus new methods and prospects were

reviewed, and in autumn of 1971 it was suggested that Oaken
Holt should be considered. When it was investigated it became
apparent that the previous owners, the National Provincial
Bank, had obtained planning permission to build a series of
permanent buildings. Seeing in this a means of providing
financial support for a Buddhist centre, Mr Saw and his
advisers went ahead with negotiations for purchase.

The purchase of Oaken Holt went through in April 1971 and
the present owners permanently moved in in September of
the same year. An added bonus to the financial situation was
that the Centre had the backing of the International Meditation
Centres, a Trust set up to aid the establishment of Buddhist
meditation techniques in the West. This institution, the IMC,
was basically responsible for the creation of Oaken Holt
Buddhist Centre, and hopes to start many more as circumstances
and finance permit.

The opening ceremony

Oaken Holt was officially opened on 4 December 1971, eight
months after the purchase deal was completed.

Mr Saw, who presided over the ceremony had the delight
of inviting seven Theravadin Buddhist monks to the occasion.
The monks recited stanzas from the Pali Canon in the Shrine
Room followed by a lecture on Buddhism. The Opening
Ceremony, which had wide and encouraging publicity in the
local press, was attended by well over 100 people from the
surrounding districts, many of whom were lay Buddhists.

Dr H. Saddhatissa acts as President of the Centre along with
his other duties as Head of the London Buddhist Vihara. The
Centre, when officially opened, was classed as a strict meditation centre, but this left the Centre with a dry and uninteresting
image. Later, this was remedied when the Ven. President
brought over two bhikkhus from Sri Lanka to set up a Vihara.
Before long, two bhikkhus arrived and took up residence in
the small cottage standing at the main entrance to the Centre.

Firstly, came Ven. K. Piyatissa, who had beforehand been Director of the Buddhist Information Centre in Colombo. His duties on arrival were and still are, the lecturing on, and instruction in Buddhist meditation and doctrine. The other bhikkhu, Ven. L. Siridhamma, who also partakes in lectures and chanting is working on a thesis on Buddhism for his doctorate, which he hopes to obtain from the nearby Oxford University. When I met the monks six years ago, I was impressed both with their enthusiasm for Western technical progress and the open help they gave me in questions on the Dharma.

The small Vihara (monastery) also serves as a dwelling for Theravadin bhikkhus 'passing through' en route to various centres throughout Britain, Europe and the Americas.

One of those bhikkhus who visited the Centre was the Ven. B. Ananda Maitreya Maha Nayaka Thera, probably the most learned and celebrated Theravadin Buddhist scholar in the East. It was my extreme pleasure to make the acquaintance of this man, a man who, amongst other things is a D Lit. of the Vidyedaya University; D Lit. of the Vidyalankara University and the Buddhist Abbot of the United Amarapura Sect of the Buddhist Church of Sri Lanka. When I met Ananda Maitreya, he wasn't in the greatest of health, and apart from his under-standably constricting English vocabulary was going slightly deaf. But with my perseverance coupled with his patient explanations, we seemed to get on rather well, and I came away from our talk more enlightened on Theravada Buddhism (which I was then studying) as well as realizing the amount of effort and will-power required to tread the Noble Eightfold Path. He emitted those rare beams of spirituality which are the direct product of insight and many, many years of medita-tion. On being questioned about the existence of Arahats in this day and age, he replied that he was convinced that there were such men walking on this planet today, but with the after-thought that such beings were very difficult to seek out, tending to embrace seclusion and anonymity. During his stay, the great Thera expounded on the nature of Nibbana before later leaving the Centre to attend the Buddhist Society's Summer School at Hoddesdon.

Meditation, as earlier explained, has become the central axis upon which the platform of a strict Buddhist life is balanced at the Centre. As a meditation centre it has some of the most ravishing country that the south of England has to offer. But as a meditation centre and retreat, it does not confine its hospitality to Buddhists. Any pilgrim, no matter what his creed, will find a kindly regard for his beliefs and lifestyle.

In those early days, accommodation was free, whilst you provided your own food and cooking facilities. If you so desired, you could donate a small sum of money for the support of the Centre. Although the Centre was open for short- and long-stay meditators, the average length of residence was usually between one and two weeks. As far as I am aware, the longest length of stay was seven weeks.

During my stay in the summer of 1973 I met an interesting fellow at the Centre. After having been shown around the Centre he was directed to his room, several doors up from mine. After initial introductions by U Myat Saw, we sat down and talked. Franz, from Switzerland, related to me that he had just returned from India after taking the Samanera (novice) vows. His bristly scalp showed that this had taken place several months previously. Having come straight from a monastery in Buddha Gaya, penniless, with few possessions, he expounded his views on the Dharma which were, to say the least, radical. In his view a bhikkhu, in order to emulate the Buddha in every respect, should be without shelter, totally abstain from book-learning and should live a life of severe renunciation of *all* attachments and find ultimate contentment in meditative reflection. Too many bhikkhus in the East, he said, spent too much time studying Pali, teaching meditation, educating the illiterate and advising politicians how to run their country's affairs; in fact anything rather than getting down to the important task of self-liberation. He then carried on and explained that when he returned to Switzerland he would don the ochre robe, travel from town to town begging alms, later bedding down for the night under a tree, and get back to living the stringent renounced life which Shakyamuni lived. I must admit, his strength of purpose and commitment were heartening, and I felt, funnily enough, a great pity for his philosophy. Somehow, wandering in the coldness of the Alps, cadging food in a country which shunned beggary and encouraged affluence, didn't seem too convincing. To my way of thinking Western countries are built on the philosophy 'from each according to his abilities, to each according to his needs',* and, incidentally, I don't hold that rigidly to the Marxist viewpoint. It's just that in this Western democracy, we must pay our way, penny by penny, even the Eightfold Path has a minimal financial sacrifice to be offered in this society.

Getting back to the Centre – not long after my visit, it became apparent that more and more people attending the Centre found a disadvantage in the cooking and eating arrangements. The main reason for this was that meditators found that the periodic involvement in obtaining, preparing and purchasing of food was restricting not only to their meditation session time limits, but the overall mindfulness developed from their meditations. The remedy lay in the hands of Sayadaw† U Rewata Dhamma of Burma, who began conducting meditation courses at the Centre in such a fashion that it became more suited to the Western environment.

U Rewata Dhamma‡ who has been in Britain since 1975, has found a comfortable and relaxed place to carry on his lectures and work in 'Oaken Holt'. He concentrates on teaching and instructing people in Vipassana meditation (i.e. insight meditation), the intensive awareness and perception of the Three Signs of Being§ in all phenomena. This, of course, is

*Karl Marx, *Critique of the Gotha Programme*.

†A Burmese term meaning the head of a group of monks; an abbot.

‡Sayadaw U Rewata Dhamma was a disciple of the Mahasi Sayadaw of Burma. He obtained his Doctorate at Benares University in Abhidhamma studies and is fully qualified to teach Abhidhamma and Buddhist philosophy.

§i.e., Dukkha, Anatta and Anicca or, Suffering, Soullessness and Impermanence.

preceded by instruction in Samatha meditation (i.e. concentrated calm or tranquillity), associated with Anapanasati, or mindfulness of breathing. The ten-day course offered at the Centre which makes comprehensive use of the two above-mentioned techniques, also includes Metta and Bhavana meditations or loving-kindness and compassion, respectively.

The Vipassana ten-day course

The daily timetable at the Centre during the course is quite exhaustive, almost austere and both physically and mentally taxing on the meditator. But what we must keep in mind is this – Enlightenment, Liberation, Self-Realization, no matter what label you stick on it, is not an expedient trapping – LSD can give one that. What we are searching for, and is amply provided in this course, is a method of self-discipline and introspection which will prove mentally lasting and will give the adept a spiritual thrust so deep into his being that the initial effect will forever be in sight of his spiritual intuition.

Arising at the early hour of 4.0 a.m., the meditator's first session commences at 4.30 and lasts until 7.0 a.m. From then until 9.0 a.m., the meditator partakes of a light breakfast, probably of grains, in the form of muesli or cereals followed by toast, cheese and tea. The second session in the Shrine Room lasts between 9.0 a.m. and 11.0 a.m., followed by lunch of vegetarian dishes. The third meditation session of the day begins at 1.0 p.m. and lasts until 4.0 p.m. Between rising from meditation and until 5.0 p.m., the meditators relax and rest in their own rooms. A light tea is then taken followed by a rest period, ending with the last session of the day at 7.0 p.m. A glass of hot milk is served after the session ends at 9.0 p.m., whereupon the meditators retire to their rooms. This adds up to a staggering nine and a half hours per day – not to be taken lightly, especially by us Westerners who find great difficulty in sitting still for any longer than ten minutes. For those readers who have been on such courses as this, it will come as no surprise in my suggesting that such a course completely 'drains' one of his or her mental and physical energy. These courses are not designed for those who dabble in 'mystical trips' and 'getting high in Vipassana'; on the contrary, it takes a dedicated and self-possessed Buddhist whose goal is Nirvana itself and not a 'joy-ride' on the 'Oriental Buddhist Express'.

Throughout the course silence is observed by everyone as a means of conserving energy which would otherwise be wasted on trivial and frivolous speech. The only times speech is directly accepted is when the meditator has his progress or problems analysed by the teacher. Each meditator has the chance of conversing with the teacher twice daily, and this is advisable even if the problem is not too pressing.

On the domestic front, food is taken sparsely, as over-eating on an intensive course such as this could prove uncomfortable, induce hallucinations and lead the meditator into drowsiness. All meals are vegetarian; apart from any ethical implications, heavy meat foods generally tend to take longer in digesting and require more precious energy which, in theory, could be utilized in meditation. As is common with most meditation centres, alcohol, smoking and drugs are absolutely prohibited. The reasons for this should be patently obvious without my explanations. Actually, many people who, although previously had been heavy smokers, have cut down considerably or even stopped smoking cigarettes as a result of daily intensive meditation. The reasons for this are that the tranquil and therapeutic effects of meditation, especially Samatha, give a balancing reaction to the nervous system thus reducing tension and restoring equanimity and calmness.

The popularity of Vipassana meditation can be witnessed by the fact that the course is now run monthly, with approximately fifty meditators enrolling for each course. The charge for the course is presently £20.00, a reasonable fee when one takes into account food, accommodation, meditation, interviews and beautiful surroundings. But I feel that the opportunity to avail oneself of the experience and knowledge of notable meditation instructors, is probably the greatest asset in this course.

The courses are attended by professional as well as working-class people, and also a small amount of people suffering from mental and psychosomatic problems attend. As stated above, the therapeutic value in meditation can cure these problems, and if not cure them, alleviates some of the stress. Vipassana meditation is similiar to growing a flower. One begins by planting the seed in the soil which has been specially treated prior to sowing. In our case the soil is the 'streamline', balancing effect of Samatha. The seed is the simple, yet, liberating tool of Vipassana. By loving care the seed is given time to germinate and is watered frequently. Slowly the stem grows, straight without flinching or bending. Again, the daily routine of sessions cultivates poise and growth, passions become controlled, thoughts are slowed down and mental activity is equalized. Then slowly the flower begins to bud, opening up its inner essence and blossoms into a many-petalled panorama of colour. The meditator, whose daily practice relieved the inner tension, begins to realize the depths and expansiveness of his omni-present being, an experience we all go through but which is incommunicable.

The course sets up no barriers to those people attending, in that it welcomes non-Buddhists to sample the liberating effect of Vipassana. Anyone can attend, whether he be black, red or yellow, no matter what his or her status in life. Throughout the course's history, people have attended from as far as the USA, Canada, Sweden, Switzerland, South America and France.

The Samanera Ordination

On 4 August 1976, Oaken Holt was chosen as a centre for an Ordination Ceremony of Samaneras to the Theravadin Sangha. To my knowledge, it was the first public Theravadin ordination of its kind. The Ceremony was conducted at the Centre following the same lines as similar occasions back in the East.

At 8.0 a.m., ten Theras* assembled in the main Shrine Room

*A Pali word connoting a bhikkhu who has been a member of the Order for over ten years.

followed by the Samaneras to be ordained. They are, at this point, still dressed as laymen. After a short prayer, each layman in turn has his hair shorn from his head and face. This begins by a tuft of hair being cut and placed in the right hand of the intending Samanera. Next, all his head is shaven followed by eyebrows and any other facial hair. Some people often ask why Buddhist monks have their heads shaven. Well, the answer to that is simple. A Buddhist monk is one who has literally renounced all material possessions and who strives for control over all sensory and mental conditions. The hair on our heads, the way we comb it, dye it, style it and cut it is a measure of one's vanity. The bhikkhu wishing to eliminate this vanity does so by the easiest and quickest method – he has his hair totally shaved off, this is the reason.

When the shaving Ceremony is completed the intending Samaneras next take a purification bath. Not just as a means of cleansing the body; more as a symbol that the layman is purifying his mind in order to do justice to the wearing of the Robe. They now return from the bath dressed in white robes, kneeling in front of the assembled Theras. Sacred texts are now recited by Theras and the intending Samaneras prior to their procession from the Shrine Room to the Dhamma Hall.

In the Dhamma Hall seated under the Buddha statue sit the Senior Monks (Theras). In front of them kneel the intending Samaneras on the raised platform. The intending Samaneras now request that they be admitted into the Order – all recitations and chanting are done in Pali. This Ceremony, along with the recitations, is exactly the same as in India two thousand years ago. The Samaneras then take their leave of the Theras, one at a time, where they discard the white robe for a yellow one – the robe of the Theravada Sangha.

When each Samanera has donned the yellow robe, they assemble before the Theras and further recitations of the sacred texts ensue, followed by the acceptance of the Vinaya Rules by the Samaneras. Between 11.00 a.m. and 12.00 noon, the Theras then leave the Dhamma Hall, followed by the Samaneras – all of whom now wear the yellow robe of the Sangha, and proceed to the Dining Hall where they take the morning, and also, the last meal of the day.

A Samanera Timetable

6.00– 7.00 a.m.	Puja and Meditation in Shrine Room
7.00– 8.00 a.m.	Morning Dana (breakfast)
9.00–11.00 a.m.	Study of the Dhamma. The senior monks each take charge of a Samanera during his period as a member of the Order of the Sangha and supervise his studies. (Pali language, Vinaya and Abhidhamma studies)
11.00–12 noon	Mid-day Dana (lunch)
12.00– 2.00 p.m.	Rest
2.00– 5.00 p.m.	Study of the Dhamma
6.00– 7.00 p.m.	Discussion and oral examination
7.00– 9.00 p.m.	Puja and Meditation in Shrine Room

The Buddhapadipa Temple

The Buddhapadipa Temple has been with us for over ten years now and was the first Thai Buddhist organization of its kind to be established in Britain. Situated in Wimbledon, the Temple, was however, first opened on 1 August 1966 at 99 Christchurch Road, East Sheen, the ceremony being conducted by Their Majesties the King and Queen of Thailand. It has been and still is, a lasting tradition in Thailand, for Royal involvement with Buddhist monastic activities and at the Buddhapadipa it is no different.

The Temple is a Theravadin institution in that it offers the teaching of the Southern School, or the Doctrine of the Elders much of its wisdom deriving from the Pali Canon.* At any one time there could be as many as ten bhikkhus in residence, some of whom are Dhammadhatu† bhikkhus. These monks

*The earliest recorded scriptures of the Theravada School, consisting of the Vinaya, the Suttas and the Abhidhamma.

†Missionary monks spreading the word of the Buddha.

live by the Patimokkha, or the 227 disciplinary rules of conduct as laid down in the Vinaya Pitaka.

In 1975, a Working Committee was established within the Temple with the express ideal of searching out larger premises, the house at East Sheen rapidly becoming inadequate to house the growing number of enquirers interested in Buddhism. That same year saw them purchase and move into the present building, formerly called Barrogill. The surroundings of the Temple are, in the summer most picturesque with a beautiful ornamental lake, complete with three beautiful wooden bridges. There is also a flower garden, a small grove with nearly every possible kind of tree that one can think of and also an orchard. It is actually a fine example of the 'proverbial English country garden' with only one difference, its situation is in the heart of South London. Also upon the four acres of land is the main building with countless number of rooms on the ground and first floors with storage and other rooms in the large attic.

There are three affiliated groups concerned with the Temple, those being the Sub-Committee for the Buddhist Mission in the UK, the Young Buddhist Association and the Lay Buddhist Association. The first of the three, the Sub-Committee for the Buddhist Mission in the UK, is made up entirely of Thais whose work it is to meet and discuss the measures necessary for furthering the Dhammadhatu work in the United Kingdom. The second group, the Young Buddhist Association, whose membership is made up mainly of Thais, work hand in hand with the Sub-Committee to arrange functions, lectures and courses at the Temple. It also looks after the daily requirements of the monks and generally aiding in the secular running of the Temple. And lastly, the third group, the Lay Buddhist Association, is made up mainly of British lay Buddhists who provide a service within the precincts of the Temple arranging courses, etc. which are open to all. The Association has an active committee of at least four, and a membership of about forty.

The history of the Temple goes back to the early sixties of the Hampstead Buddhist Vihara, when the incumbent monk was a Canadian called Ananda Bodhi. The English Sangha Trust at Haverstock Hill invited at this time Ananda Bodhi's teacher Chao Khun Rajasiddhimuni from Thailand. He duly arrived in England around 1964 with his interpreter Phra Maha Vichitt.

In 1964, Phra Maha Vichitt moved into a house at 99 Christchurch Road, East Sheen, London and was officially opened two years later as the Buddhapadipa Temple. The Temple was opened as a meditation centre and attracted many Europeans. Subsequently, Maha Vichitt himself attracted a large following.

A year later, Vichitt was joined at the Temple by two further bhikkhus from Thailand, Phra Maha Vorasak and Phra Maha Boonchuay. With the coming of these monks, the Temple began to flourish and was probably one of the most important Theravadin centres in Europe. It certainly had these outstanding meditation teachers, and meditation was fast becoming a sought-after acquisition. By 1969, two other meditation centres were opening up, one in Biddulph, Cheshire, the other at Hindhead under *Phra Maha Vichitt who had been promoted and was now known as Chao Khun Sobhana Dhammasudhi. Under Chao Khun Sobhana, the guidance and teaching received by his pupils led them to form a lay group known as the Buddhapadipa Temple Fellowship.

In 1969, Vorasak and Boonchuay left the Temple and went to university and Chao Khun Sobhana disrobed. However, before going to university, Phra Maha Boonchuay felt that a lay association should be formed (the earlier Temple Fellowship was already defunct) hence, in 1969, Maha Boonchuay established the Lay Buddhist Association and was consequently its first President with Roy Brabant-Smith as its Chairman.

The main purpose of the Lay Buddhist Association as laid down in its rules are basically to keep the Precepts, to practise meditation, follow and propagate the Dhamma and to help, in any way possible, the monks at the Temple. The Association

*Dhammasudhi has since disrobed and is now known as Dhiravamsa and is the Meditation Master of his own Centre at Chapter House, Wisbech.

also runs classes of its own as well as arranging major functions such as Vesakha Day,* Asalha Puja Day,† and Magha Puja Day.‡ Another function of the Association which has proven invaluable has been aiding the monks with their English. This has led to an improvement in the talks and lessons given by the monks to the laity.

The Lay Buddhist Association is presently engaged in a Saturday and Sunday programme of meditation and talks at the Temple which are giving newcomers to Buddhism the chance to get accustomed to the teachings of the Lord Buddha from the Theravada standpoint. On Saturdays classes commence at 3.00 p.m. and consist approximately of one and a half hours' walking and sitting meditation followed by a discussion over tea. Spiritual guidance and meditation instructions are given, if necessary, by the Temple's Meditation Teacher, Phra Khun Palad. Sunday meetings commence in the afternoons with two hours' walking and sitting meditation preceded by the taking of the Precepts (Pancasila) and interspersed with chanting. There is then a further class at 5.30 p.m. which includes meditation and a talk followed by discussion.

After three years at Wimbledon Parkside, the Buddhapadipa now looks substantially quite sound and with all things going well a new, but smaller Temple, built in the same style as traditional Thai architecture, is in the offing. It should be remembered that the Buddhapadipa Temple is *not* a short- or long-term residential centre for lay-Buddhists, whether they be Thai or not. The Temple is a refuge, as it were, for Thai monks of the Theravada school and opens its doors only for meditation sessions and lectures.

---

*The most important day of the Buddhist calendar – the ceremonial commemoration of the Buddha's birth, Enlightenment and decease.

†Commemorates the Buddha's renunciation.

‡Commemorates the conferment of two of his closest disciples – Moggallana and Sariputta.

The Buddhapadipa week-day schedule

Monday:	6.00 a.m.–7.00 a.m.	Puja and meditation
	6.00 p.m.–7.00 p.m.	Puja and meditation
Tuesday:	6.00 a.m.–7.00 a.m.	Puja and meditation
	6.00 p.m.–7.00 p.m.	Puja and meditation
	7.30 p.m.–9.00 p.m.	Meditation (1 hr) followed by a talk and discussion
Wednesday:	6.00 a.m.–7.00 a.m.	Puja and meditation
	6.00 p.m.–7.00 p.m.	Puja and meditation
Thursday:	6.00 a.m.–7.00 a.m.	Puja and meditation
	6.00 p.m.–7.00 p.m.	Puja and meditation
Friday:	6.00 a.m.–7.00 a.m.	Puja and meditation
	6.00 p.m.–7.00 p.m.	Puja and meditation

Shades of Dhamma

Taking refuge in the Triple Gem

The basic foundation and, incidentally, the most elemental undertaking of *any* Buddhist is his taking refuge in the Buddha, the Dhamma and the Sangha or, the Triple Gem. When we take refuge in the Triple Gem, we are making an individual sustained effort to put into practice the principles of Buddhism laid down by Shakyamuni in his teaching or Dhamma, and draw strength from the community of monks, the Sangha who have lived and been liberated by these principles.

The Buddha

To take refuge in the Bhudda is to understand completely that Shakyamuni, after many lifetimes, awakened to the truth of suffering through his own efforts, and because of his limitless compassion for mankind, proclaimed the eternal, indestructible Dhamma. The Buddha is seen to be a paragon of virtue, wisdom and Enlightenment and should be venerated, not as a God, however, but as one who has pierced the veil of ignorance and delusion and, for that very reason we take refuge in Him.

The Dhamma

For the forty-five years of his ministry after the Great Enlightenment, Gautama tirelessly spread the Dhamma. His teachings consisted of the highest moral, psychological and philosophical achievements, unparalleled in the history of religion. Through a properly ordered moral life, coupled with the daily practice of meditation, the Buddha prophesied liberation in the personal experience of Nibbana. But only through constant mental and ethical development could this be achieved hence, we take refuge in the Dhamma.

The Sangha

The community of monks or bhikkhus make up the Sangha, the last of the Refuges. The Sangha is comprised totally of men and, in various Mahayana schools, of women who have relinquished the life of luxury and possessions for the life of poverty, renunciation and meditation. The austerity of this lifestyle is well known and demands the utmost conviction from the monk desirous of emulating the Buddha in body, mind and speech. They live by the Patimokkha which, if adhered to passionately, engenders such virtue and respect which we should salute; so we take refuge in the Sangha.

Salutation to the Buddha, Dhamma and Sangha

Such indeed, is that Blessed One; Worthy,
Omniscient, Endowed with knowledge and virtue,
Well-gone, Knower of worlds, an Incomparable
Charioteer for the training of persons, Teacher
of gods and men, Enlightened and Blessed.

Well-expounded is the Dhamma by the Lord;
To be realized; with immediate fruit;
Inviting investigation; leading on to
Nibbana; to be completely comprehended by
the wise, each for himself.

Of good conduct is the Order of the Disciples
of the Blessed One; of upright conduct is the
Order of the Disciples of the Blessed One; of
wise conduct is the Order of the Disciples of
the Blessed One; of dutiful conduct is the
Order of the Disciples of the Blessed One. This
Order of the Disciples of the Blessed One – namely,
those four pairs of persons, the Eight Kinds
of individuals – is worthy of offerings, is worthy
of hospitality, is worthy of gifts, is worthy of
reverential salutations, is an uncomparable field
of merit to the world.

The Refuge Formula and its translation

Namo Tassa Bhagavato Arahato Sammasambuddhassa (repeat thrice).
Homage to the Blessed One, the Arahant, the Fully Enlightened
One.

> *Buddham Saranam Gacchami,*
> *Dhamman Saranam Gacchami,*
> *Sangham Saranam Gacchami.*

I take in refuge in Buddha,
I take in refuge in Dhamma,
I take refuge in the Sangha.

> *Dutiyampi Buddham Saranam Gacchami,*
> *Dutiyampi Dhamman Saranam Gacchami,*
> *Dutiyampi Sangham Saranam Gacchami.*

For the second time I take refuge in the Buddha,
For the second time I take refuge in the Dhamma,
For the second time I take refuge in the Sangha.

> *Tatiyampi Buddham Saranam Gacchami,*
> *Tatiyampi Dhammam Saranam Gacchami,*
> *Tatiyampi Sangham Saranam Gacchami.*

For the third time I take refuge in the Buddha,
For the third time I take refuge in the Dhamma,
For the third time I take refuge in the Sangha.

Devotion in the Shrine Room

The Shrine Room in any temple or monastery should be considered holy ground, apart from the fact that it might contain relics of the Buddha. One should always enter a shrine room minus footwear and present oneself before the Buddharupa. The shrine itself accommodates the Buddharupa as the central axis with various receptacles, incense burners, flower vases, small rupas, and other devotional implements resplendent on either side. On arrival in front of the shrine one should prostrate oneself thrice in salutation to the Triple Gem. This is done by placing the hands in Anjali (the bringing together of the hands in a prayer-like fashion at breast level). Squatting on, one's knees, one should proceed to bow and touch the forehead on the floor, the hands extended on either side of the head, simultaneously repeating the Tisarana, i.e. I take refuge in the Buddha, etc., etc.

It has been a traditional practice in Theravada Buddhism to proffer offerings of food, water, lights and incense to the Shrine, dedicating them to the Triple Gem. This again can be done simultaneously reciting short salutations in the process. In Buddhism a comprehensive word to cover all these foregoing practices is Puja, literally meaning 'paying homage.' These exercises can be proceeded by group meditation and finally the recitation of either the Jayamangala Gatha or the Mahajaya-mangala Gatha, or the Ratana, Karaniya or Metta suttas. The preliminary meditations in the Theravada school generally are the practice of mettabhavana, or loving kindness; anapanasati, or the mindfulness of breathing; satipatthana, or the contemplations of the body, feelings, the mind and the mental contents. This meditation is, however, of a higher nature leading to the development of insight, also known by its popular name of Vipassana (insight meditation).

The British Buddhist Association

The British Buddhist Association is yet another unique entity in the current British Buddhist scene. The Association is basically and, I might add, the only organization in Britain where one may study, part time, the Buddhist teachings in an academic way under scholastic conditions. This is a much needed organization, even although it tends to concentrate on Theravada doctrine, hence its inclusion in this chapter. However, as you will see later, it also incorporates a few Mahayana themes in its comprehensive syllabus.

The Association was officially opened on Vesakha Day (8 May) 1974 when a ceremony was held at Elgin Mansions, London. The ceremony took the form of a Buddhist Devotional Service followed by a lecture on the Buddhist way of life by the Ven. Dr M. Vajiragnana, MA, DLITT, the Association's Religious Director and was brought to a close by a short meditation. On that memorable occasion Mr A. Haviland Nye, FCA (Administrative Director), Mrs I. R. Quittner (Honorary Associate) and Mr Russell Webb (Hon. Secretary British Mahabodhi Society) were in attendance, to mention but a few.

Shortly after its establishment, the Association drew up a list of objects which they committed themselves to promote and uphold; they were briefly:

1 To provide systematic instruction in the Dhamma, primarily based on Pali source materials.
2 To promote Canonical, textual and linguistic studies.
3 To advise upon matters relating to the Dhamma, its practice, study and literature.
4 To maintain close contact with individuals and groups in the West interested in promoting and supporting the foregoing aims.

From the aforesaid it would seem as though the Association was purely an educational body. Well, to a certain extent this is true as can be gleaned from the courses outlined later in this section. But the Association also provides another vital and communal service – that of a religious body. This has occurred basically because of the nature of the subjects studied by the student. Students, who, after much study and discernment of the teachings, find it increasingly more beneficial to their studies if they carry out the work and assignments with the objective of leading a full Buddhist life on completion of their studies. An ever deepening comprehension of the Buddha's teachings sometimes makes this inevitable – but no one is complaining, least of all the student. To embrace the Buddhist life is indeed a noble quest and the BBA courses fulfil this need in a most encyclopaedic way. But this is not to say that one has to be a Buddhist to study with the BBA, anybody can enrol, no matter his creed, as the teachings are presented in a plain and consistent way intelligible to anybody. Obviously a Buddhist organization like the BBA is not likely to confine its functions and business to the purely academic. This can be seen by the fact that it occupies an Arama (Temple) at Crowndale Road, Camden, which incidentally, is the private address of Ven. Vajiragnana. The Association's main office is at Hatton Garden and also draws support from the Working Men's College where the educational side of the BBA takes place in the form of lectures and classes. As mentioned elsewhere, the BBA is basically a Theravada institution, they 'follow the Buddha's school' and are a distinctively British Buddhist organization. The main bulk of the teaching comes from the Pali Canon, the earliest recorded words and discourses of the Buddha Shakyamuni.

Over the years the Association has attracted a growing number of students, most of whom are Buddhists and the last figure quoted to me by Ven. Vajiragnana was approximately one hundred, but I assume that this figure has increased because of the applications for enrolment I was shown the last time I met Ven. Vajiragnana. This is a most encouraging sign reinforced by the fact that many students still keep ties with the Association after completing the Basic Buddhism Course and from time to time come back for further advanced study.

For those who see the BBA as a means ‚to studying the Buddha's teaching with the aim of continuing his or her commitment to Buddhism by either becoming a lay Buddhist or by becoming a Supporter of the BBA, the Association has listed three stages in the pursuance of this ideal:

Part 1: Introductory Course.
Part 2: Preparation through further study and Puja.
Part 3: Commitment to Meditation Course.

As Parts 2 and 3 are, to a great extent, of a personal and hence private affair, the author finds it more informative if Part 1 is looked at in detail as the means whereby one continues further study and commitment.

The BBA Basic Buddhism Course

The Association's Basic Buddhism Course is an extensive series of lectures* dealing with all areas of Buddhism and gives the student a thorough grounding in which to base deeper studies in more exacting doctrines. This can be easily undertaken by the Association's specialized courses such as its Abhidhamma and Pali language courses. Each of the seven parts of the course are divided into six-week blocks, which, when holidays are included, lasts about the same length of time as the normal academic year. But I should just reiterate that all classes are part-time and, as yet, there are no official certificates awarded on completion of the course. From a spiritual and mental point of view, the student gains possibly more than can be offered by a piece of paper with someone's signature on it – a higher understanding of himself and his surroundings.

As with all courses of study, no matter what the content, one is required to buy and to study various reading assignments. The BBA is no different, most of the assignments coming from individual Buddhist authorities, suttas and Buddhist Publication Society publications (*Wheel* series).

Part 1 Introduction

Part 1 is divided up into five main parts:

*These are more discussion classes than teacher/pupil lectures.

1 Introduction
2 Knowledge
3 Mind
4 The Four Noble Truths
4a Rebirth
4b The Third and Fourth Noble Truths
5 Meditation

From the above it can be seen that this course deals in the main with basic Buddhist doctrines. An introduction sets out the details of the course and the aims of the Association and the Buddhist life in general. Knowledge and Mind, two vital sectors of Buddhist philosophy are studied along with the important doctrines of the Four Noble Truths, the *raison d'être* of all consequent Buddhist thought. An introduction to meditation and its goals are included in this preliminary course.

Part 2 (a) Buddhist Psychology

Part 2 is divided up into eight separate courses and provides the student with specialized segments of the whole panorama of Buddhist thought and culture.

1 The dynamic faculties of mental phenomena, mundane and transcendental
2 Processes of cognition; kamma and its resultants
3 Citta (consciousness); ethical division of mental framework; expansion of consciousness into four spheres
4 Citta (cont.): Psychological roots; feelings; spontaneity of thought; knowledge
5 Cetasikas (Mental concomitants): basic qualities of mental activity
6 Cetasikas (cont.): cultivation of basic qualities for mental development (bhavana)

Reading Assignment:
The Psychology and Philosophy of Buddhism, Dr W. F. Jayasuriya.

This course sets out to define and examine the mind in all

its entirety, from the basic functions of cognition to the highest level of mental development. This is a continuation of lesson 2 Part I and forms a foundation for the yet higher teachings as expounded in the Abhidhamma.

Part 2 (b) Rebirth and causation

This part of the course deals with the all important theory of Rebirth and Causation. Both parts are broken up into two three-weekly courses:

Rebirth
1   Rebirth in Western thought; Henry Ford, Lloyd-George, Tolstoy, Wagner, Voltaire, Hume, Spinoza, Leibniz, Plato, Pythagoras and others
2   Recall of memories from previous lives: case study
3   Buddhist theory of how rebirth functions

Causation
4   The Tibetan Wheel of Life, death and rebirth through the six realms
5   Conditioned genesis; ways of penetrating the Wheel; transcending passion and wrong views
6   Multiplicity of conditions in the arising of material and mental phenomena

*Reading assignments**
The Case for Rebirth, Francis Story
Survival and Karma, K. N. Jayatilleke
Rebirth Explained, V. F. Gunaratna
The Wheel of Birth and Death, Ven. Kantipalo
Dependent Origination, Ven. Piyadassi
The Significance of Dependent Origination, Ven. Nyanitiloka

Here is the study of one of those controversial subjects not only limited to the field of Buddhism. As can be seen from the first lesson Part 2 (b)1, the student briefly looks at some of

*All *Wheel* series booklet publications.

the experiences and stories of Western writers and thinkers. The whole causative chain of dependent origination is studied in depth along with the Wheel of Life and Tibetan Buddhism, a picturesque presentation of this fascinating philosophy.

Part 2 (c) Buddhist ethical conduct

This six-week course is again divided into weekly lessons dealing with the whole sphere of Buddhist morality:

1	Buddhist conduct as part of bhavana, the basis of ethical theory; freedom; survival; kamma; nibbana and the teleological nature of Buddhist Ethics
2	Significance of the Refuges and Precepts skilful and unwholesome actions
3	Personal relationships; Sigalovada Sutta
4 & 5	Buddhist attitudes and conduct in modern industrialized society
6	The monks' Vinaya (disciplinary or canon law); origin: Vinaya Pitaka; practice

Reading assignments:
Buddhist Ethics: Essence of Buddhism, Ven. Dr H. Saddhatissa
The Ethics of Buddhism, S. Tachibana

This course outlines the role played by morality in the Eightfold Path of the Buddha. It is said that in order to be able to progress in the higher stages of the Buddhist life, the student must firstly understand his various obligations to society. Only then is he ready for any kind of mental and contemplative development.

Part 2 (d) Life of the Buddha

1 Sources of knowledge; the Buddha's ancestors, family and early life; geography of early Buddhism; political, social and economic life

D

2 Four signs; Great Renunciation; austerities; yogic teachers
   and the Five; Enlightenment and the seven weeks there-
   after
3 Preaching; the Five as disciples; Yasa and his associates; the
   Sangha; daily routines; rainy seasons; the first twenty years'
   ministry
4 Chief disciples; main supporters; Devadatta's schism
5 The last days; mahaparinibbana; First Council
6 Previous Buddhas; the Bodhisattva and practice of the
   Perfections

Reading assignments
The Life of the Buddha as Legend and History, E. J. Thomas

This course sets out the life of the Buddha, his renunciation
from worldly ties and the teaching he offered to the world as
a result of his Enlightenment experience.

Part 2 (e) Buddhist Meditation

The fifth course of Part 2 deals with the subject of meditation
as found in the *Satipatthana Sutta*, probably the most authoritative work to be found in the whole of Theravadin Buddhist
literature:

1 Introduction: problems of translation etc: kinds of meditation
2 Mindfulness as to Body
3 Mindfulness as to Feelings
4 Mindfulness as to States of Mind
5 Mindfulness as to Dhammas (Mind-Objects)
6 Conclusion

Reading assignments
The Heart of Buddhist Meditation, Ven. Nyaniponika Thera
Middle Length Sayings, no. 10 ⎱ see Pali Canon
Digha Nikaya, no. 22 ⎰

As meditation is a vast subject in Buddhism, the student is advised to read and to compare various books on the subject as a means to understand, at least partially, why the subject is so vital in comprehending the Buddha's teaching. But meditation is ultimately something one does and not a topic for discussion.

Part 2 (f) History of Buddhism in India

1 Society, philosophy and religion at the time of the Buddha
2 Continuation of Part II (f)1
3 The Councils; establishing the Pali Canon; the early schools
4 Mahayana I: The Bodhisattva – the ten Paramitas devotion and faith
5 Mahayana II: Sunyata and the Madhyamika school; Nagarjuna
6 Mahayana III: Yogacara and Asanga; the Trikaya

Reading assignments
The History of Buddhist Thought, E. J. Thomas

This enormous subject is broken up into two particular areas of thought. Firstly the student studies the immediate future after the Buddha's Parinibbana and the problems and the inevitable schisms which took place within the Sangha. Following on from this is the rise of the Mahayana Vehicle with its own brand of philosophy and thought crystallized in the form of the Bodhisattva and the cultivation of the Ten Paramitas (perfections). Lastly, the student studies the lives of some of India's greatest exponents on the Mahayana path and the doctrines they propounded.

Part 2 (g) Buddhist sects

The seventh course deals with the rise and history of some of the later forms of Buddhism as formulated in Tibet and the Far East.

1 Roots of Tibetan Buddhism in Indian Mahayana; the three Yanas
2 Developed forms of Tibetan Buddhism; Ati Yoga
3 History of Cha'an and Zen Buddhism in China and Japan
4 Rinzai and Soto Zen; the Koan and Zazen
5 Origins of Pure Land Buddhism
6 Practice of Pure Land Buddhism

Reading assignments

The assignments for this particular course are recommended by the class tutor according to the progress made by the individual and/or the class.

In this course the student is introduced to the many sects non-Theravadin where a brief study of each sect's meditation techniques are examined and compared.

The Association is presently drawing up a prospectus for Part 2 (h) Buddhist Art, which, it is hoped, will be included as part of the course in the near future.

The Association, which has steadily grown since its inception back in 1974, currently has something like eighteen tutors, both visiting and guest, who offer their services. Some come from Working Men's College and a few are presently university lecturers. The principal tutors within the Association are Ven. Vajiragnana, Mr George Robertson and Mr A. Haviland-Nye. The Zen, Tibetan and Shingon classes were first conducted by Dr Irmgard Schloegl and Trevor Leggett, Michael Hookham and Rev. Jack Austin respectively.

Apart from the Arama and Working Men's College, both in Camden, the BBA have held classes at various locations in London the most popular being at the Meeting House, Hampstead and at Gentle Ghost as well as introductory courses at Seymour Hall and at St Martin's Lane.

With so many financial transactions and administrative burdens, it will be appreciated that the Association, like every other Buddhist organization in Britain, requires a fair deal of

money in order to survive. As can be assumed, the large quantity of this money comes from students' contributions. However, the Association has a number of supporters (Dayakas-male
and Dayikas-female) who finance numerous activities by
monthly contributions. One need not be a Buddhist to
become a supporter and absolutely no religious commitment is
involved. Nevertheless, the majority of supporters are lay-
Buddhists and enjoy a communal atmosphere within the
Association and can derive, if so desired, personal spiritual help
from the Religious Director.

The Association is also, as mentioned elsewhere, a religious
body and celebrates all the usual Buddhist festivals during
the year, especially Vesakha Day. Meditation sessions are also
held at the Arama (Crowndale Road) on Saturdays and Sundays. This usually requires the meditator to take Refuge and
to recite the Panca Sila.* Offerings of flowers, incense and
lights are given (Dana) in grand salutation of the Buddha,
Dhamma and Sangha. Sitting meditation is conducted ranging
from anapanasati (mindfulness of breathing) to mettabhavana
(meditation on loving-kindness).

The British Buddhist Association is one of those valuable
institutions much required by us in the West where scholastic
studies in technology have been given preference and pride of
place in our society. It is both refreshing and indeed crucial
that an academic institution like the BBA is promoting Buddhist studies of the highest level, and where the teachings of
Buddhism can be so readily acquired. Long may it continue.

Addendum: Dhammapadipa
(The Hampstead Buddhist Vihara)

There have been several attempts to establish a purely English
or Western Theravadin Buddhist Sangha over the past fifty

*The Five Precepts as observed by the layman: non-killing; non-stealing;
avoidance of sexual misconduct; non-lying; and avoidance of consuming
intoxicating drink and drugs.

years in England, the original idea being the brainchild of the late Anagarika Dharmapala. A Sangha, living strictly by all 227 rules of the Patimokkha in the West is no mean feat as was witnessed when the Hampstead Buddhist Vihara came into being. However, all this took place when, in 1956, the English Sangha Trust was established with the firm intention of forming an actual Theravadin Sangha in England. This was the major preoccupation of one man, William Purfurst. Purfurst had earlier received the novice ordination under the Ven. Sayadaw U Thittila as the Samanera Dhammananda. In 1954 he travelled to Thailand with several disciples and was duly ordained into the Sangha as Bhikkhu Kapilavaddho at Wat Paknam in Bangkok.

After his arrival back in England two years later, Bhikkhu Kapilavaddho set about forming the English Sangha Trust with premises at 50 Alexandra Road, Swiss Cottage. A supporters' group was also created and known as the English Sangha Association. The Association, apart from its role of maintaining the monks, etc., published a monthly periodical called *Sangha*.

In 1957, because of deteriorating health, the Ven. Kapilavaddho disrobed, and one of his closest followers, the Ven. Pannavaddho (Peter Morgan) succeeded him. For several years the Ven. Pannavaddho attempted gallantly to direct the affairs of the Association as well as practising and teaching Dhamma. Attempts to recruit new members of the Sangha and retain them were not very successful, and for a great part of the time the Ven. Pannavaddho virtually carried on single-handed. During this period, therefore, an English Sangha cannot have been said to exist. Finally, the Ven. Pannavaddho returned to Thailand to continue his training under the Ven. Acharn Maha Boowa at Wat Barn Tard, near Udorn Thani.

On 28 October 1962 the Hampstead Buddhist Vihara was officially opened at 131 Haverstock Hill, NW3, under the auspices of the English Sangha Trust. This was the second major attempt to achieve the objectives of the Trust and to establish a sound Theravadin Sangha. This second attempt was further consolidated when the Ven. Kapilavaddho, having been re-ordained at Wat Buddhapadipa at East Sheen, returned to take command of his former post. His verve and energy were a marked characteristic, and for a time the nucleus of a Sangha seemed to be taking shape. In October 1968, on the occasion of a visit by the Vice-Patriarch of Thailand, the Vihara was renamed Dhammapadipa. However, in 1971 the Ven. Kapilavaddho died, having previously disrobed again because of failing health and his foremost pupil, Alan James (formerly Ven. Dipadhammo) struggled on himself to preserve some of the prestige built up by his teacher. The Vihara endured for some time on a lay basis but finally petered out through lack of direction and monastic commitment.

After five years of virtual inactivity a fresh chapter unfolded when Mr George Sharp, the Chairman of the Trust, visited Thailand. There he met a distinguished meditation teacher, the Ven. Acharn Cha, Abbot of Wat Ba Pong, and asked for advice and guidance about the Vihara. After consultations, the Abbot visited England in May 1977 and set about the formation of a Sangha at the Vihara – the third attempt! He unfortunately had to return to Thailand in July 1977 owing to the many duties back at his own temple. But before leaving he placed the Vihara under the care of an American monk, the Ven. Acharn Sumedho.

This latest development is proving most popular, and hopeful prospects for the future are forecast. At the Vihara are now three other bhikkhus, Ven. Khemadhammo (English), Ven. Anando (American) and Ven. Viriyadhammo (Canadian), and a completely Western Theravadin Sangha is beginning to assert itself. Dhammapadipa has since been attracting steadily growing numbers of people to its meditation sessions which, by the way, are held daily at 5 a.m. and 7 a.m. There are also encouraging signs that the Sangha at the Vihara will expand as candidates for ordination present themselves. And now, after twenty-two years of ups and downs, it can be seen that a solidarity of commitment on a lay, as well as monastic basis, is strengthening. Plans are currently being made for a move to premises in the country to enable the Sangha to expand and develop under more suitable conditions.

A sister Vihara, under the guidance of the Ven. Acharn Cha, has recently been opened at Tournon, near Valence, in France.

5 The Multi-Coloured Mandala – Tibet in Britain

The Kagyu Samye-Ling Tibetan Centre

When the Iron Bird flies and horses run on wheels, the Tibetan
people will be scattered like ants across the world and the Dharma
will come to the land of the Red Man.

PADMASAMBHAVA, *eighth century*

Samye-Ling, a unique feature of British Buddhism has been
with us for over ten years – a decade in which this hitherto
unknown entity has blossomed into an international Tibetan
Buddhist Centre, and is now seen by many to be a serious
vessel for the proclamation of Tibetan Buddhist teachings in
Europe.

Lying a couple of miles north of the small village of Eskdalemuir which, incidentally, enjoys the worst and the best of
weather conditions in Britain, Samye-Ling remains almost
enveloped by every kind of tree and shrub one can think of.
This twenty-five-room mansion situated on twenty-three
acres of land with the River Esk forming a boundary, provides
the serious lay Buddhist and any other pilgrim following a
Sadhana, all the requisite surroundings for peaceful meditation
and study. The undisturbed beauty, only ever broken by the
odd jet passing overhead, instills in one a unity with nature,
a compassionate brotherly attitude towards one's fellow men
and a verve and confidence for one's goal which can be so

hard to achieve 'in the world'. Coupled with this is the direction and teaching of visiting lamas and meditation teachers which makes for a profitable stay as worthwhile as anything being offered anywhere in Europe.

The Centre, however, used to operate as the Johnstone House Meditation Centre under the control of one Ananda Bodhi, now Namgyal Rimpoche. But back in 1967 two Tibetan Rimpoches, Vens. Shetrop Akong Tarap and Chogyam Trungpa Rimpoche took an active interest in securing Johnstone House for establishing a Tibetan centre in Europe.

Chogyam Trungpa met Akong Tarap whilst the latter was the then Abbot of the monastery of Drolma Lhakhang in the eastern province of Kham. It was here that the two Rimpoches contrived to flee Tibet with the insurgence of the Red Communist armies. Akong, whilst still young, was soon recognized as a 'tulku'* and was brought to the above-mentioned monastery to re-continue his previous life's work.† Both Rimpoches follow the lineage of Kagyudpa mystics which goes back to the Celestial Buddha Dorje Chang (Dharmakaya Vajradhara), more of which will be explained later.

On their arrival in North India it was decided that the dissolution of Tibetan traditions and religion was now irrefragable and that the future of Tibetan Buddhism now lay in North India (Nepal, Bhutan and Sikkim) and more importantly in the West. There are those who see in this affair an auspicious sign that the wisdom and 'magic' of Tibet should be disseminated to the world as the last tracings of the ancient mystical teachings of our forefathers.

When they arrived in England from India both Rimpoches, although still sharing their common goal, temporarily went their different ways. Chogyam Trungpa, with a view to teach and write of the Dharma in the West, took a scholarship in

---

*A 'tulku' is taken as a recognized incarnation, usually the Abbot or head of an important monastery. The most revered tulku of course is the Dalai Lama, the only one of some three hundred 'official' incarnations.

†The flight from Tibet is recorded in Chogyam Trungpa's *Born in Tibet* Allen and Unwin, London, 1971.

English at St Anthony's College, Oxford. Akong Tarap, similarly taking up the study of English, decided to commence work in a hospital in Oxford which would enhance his already considerable knowledge of Tibetan medicine. Because of the interest and enthusiasm shown by Buddhists in this area, it was decided that a meditation group should be formed in Oxford. This group met regularly on Sunday mornings with Chogyam Trungpa as meditation leader and adviser.

It was in 1967 that they decided that a more permanent centre should be formed, an institution where some of the cultural and spiritual heritage of Tibet could be preserved in all its entirety, and which would stand as a crossroads for East–West cultural and traditional exchange. Chogyam Trungpa who by now was lecturing in many countries throughout Europe and whose reputation as a meditation teacher was by now widespread, was invited by Ananda Bodhi to begin a series of lectures at Johnstone House. He saw in Johnstone House a beautiful refuge and an excellent centre in which Tibetan culture could be preserved. With the aid of the Johnstone House Trust, the mansion was purchased and was reborn Samye-Ling Tibetan Centre. The Centre was named after the first great Buddhist monastery/university of Samye, founded in the ninth century AD by Padmasambhava.

The centre is dedicated to the upholding of the Kagyudpa school of Tibetan Buddhism, its doors remaining open to all religious, philosophical and theological schools of thought and welcomes each with unimpeded warmth. The first time I stayed there, it was my pleasure to make aquaintance with many pilgrims of one school and another, many having travelled the world over in search of spiritual Truth. But one of the apparent features which astonished me was the coming and going of people – Japanese, American, Canadian and yet another dozen nationalities. The house continually exuded of an admixture of the finest incense and a crystal clear tranquillity. Some came 'to get away from it all', some to study, some to write their theses and others to make retreat. But the largest percentage came feeling the need for entire seclusion and retire for a period of intensive meditation. Unlike many other Buddhist centres in Britain, Samye-Ling holds no one to a set pattern, but allows one to simply do one's own thing in one's own way.

The spiritual head of the centre is His Holiness, the Gyalwa Karmapa, the leader of the Kagyudpa School. Amongst the high ranking lamas who have been, and still are, associated with the Centre are the Very Ven. Kalu Rimpoche, Ven. Chogyam Trungpa Rimpoche, Ven. Chime Rimpoche and the Ven. Ato Rimpoche. The Administrator at the Centre is the Ven. Akong Tarap Rimpoche, whom we have established as a Co-Founder.

The Gyalwa Karmapa and the Kagyudpa lineage

The Kagyudpa school of Tibetan Buddhism* derives its philosophy from the Sunyavadins, who emphasized the metaphysical aspect of 'sunyata' (The Great Void) in all compositions, which later found an ideal expression in the Vajrayana. The ancestral line dates back to the great yogi Milarepa (AD 1052–1135), probably the greatest and most evolved Tibetan yogi ever. Milarepa's guru, Marpa – the Translator, received the esoteric doctrine from an Indian Tantrist called Naropa, who in turn transmitted the secret oral teachings of the Demchog-Tantra (The Mandala of Highest Bliss) and his famous 'Six Doctrines'† to his disciple Marpa. To complete the 'patriarchal' line, Naropa's teacher Tilopa (*c.* AD 975) who, it is said, inherited the divine teaching of a Mahamudra (the Great Symbol) meditation from the Celestial Buddha of the Kagyudpa, Vajradhara.

The first Karmapa (Detson Khenpo), who was a disciple to Cho Je Gampopa, who in turn was the chief disciple of

*Apart from the Kagyudpa, the other three schools of Tibetan Buddhism are the Sakya, Nyingmapa and Gelugpa.

†The 'Six Doctrines' are briefly: The Doctrines of Inner Fire (gtum-mo); of the Illusory Body (Sgyu-lus); of the Dream State (rmi-lam); of the Clear Light (lod-gsal); of the Intermediate State (bar-do); of the Transference of Consciousness (lpho-ba).

Milarepa, spread the teachings in Tibet on a scale never before attempted (AD 1100). He established seats of learning in Eastern and Central Tibet and founded the principal seat of the Karmapas at Tsurphu. The Karmapa lineage is inundated with tales and miracles of the teachings and at the power of some of the tulkus.

The second Karmapa, for instance, called Karmapakshi, managed to convince the Taoists of the greatness and sublimity of the Buddhadharma. The presents offered to him on his travels he threw into a nearby fountain at Shang Tu in China. However, the mystical power of the Karmapa was evinced when the same presents turned up at a pool near the monastery he resided in at Tsurphu.

The present Karmapa, the sixteenth to date, was born in the Eastern province of Kham in the year 1923, near the Gold Water River. In his previous incarnation* he predicted the place and date of his birth and also the family he was destined to join. Such was his holiness that he could be heard to recite the sacred mantra 'Om Mani Padme Hum' whilst still in his mother's womb!

The great birth took place on the fifteenth day of the sixth Tibetan month in the year of the Wood Mouse, at a spot called Sange Namzona. Celestial music resounded along with the emanations of the colours of the rainbow which surrounded the tent in which he was born. Later, the Situ Rimpoche, Padma Wangchuk arrived with two other Rimpoches and on glancing at the body identified him as the sixteenth Karmapa.

At the age of eight, and after formal recognition by the thirteenth Dalai Lama, the young Karmapa returned to his monastery at Tsurphu to undergo his philosophical, religious and Tantric training. When he was thirteen years old he left Tsurphu and embarked on a journey to Palpung in Kham, performing miracles along the way. When he arrived at Palpung he studied the secret doctrines under the Situ Rimpoche. His guru initiated him into the higher Tantric practices

*The fifteenth-century Karmapa, Khayab Dorje, 1871–1922.

and meditative techniques until he was eighteen, whereupon he left Kham and returned to Tsurphu.

During the years 1952 to 1953 he accompanied the Dalai Lama on a visit to China. When he arrived back in Tibet both went on a pilgrimage visiting all the monastic centres in Kham. Within the next three years he devoted much of his time and energy in the re-organization and re-building of the seat of the Karmapas ar Tsurphu.

His divine vision, a manifestation of his omniscience and boundless compassion, perceived the catalytic future of his country and fled like so many other lamas into India. The Maharaja of Sikkim, seeing the futility of the Karmapa's plight, offered him land near the old Rumtek monastery, close to the capital Gangtok, where a new monastery was built to house the entourage along with their many scriptures, relics and ceremonial articles. It is from this new centre that the Karmapa now lives, teaches and organizes his many journeys across the globe.

At the present time Akong still remains Administrator and meditation adviser, Sherapalden Beru continues to turn out magnificent thanka paintings and, lastly, Ven. Samten Zeau is still meditation and Puja leader.

Anyone wishing to begin a life of Buddhist practice in the Tibetan tradition will find a most comforting and encouraging atmosphere at Samye-Ling. For instance, the Shrine Room itself is the most beautiful and aesthetic I have ever seen. But then colour, form, symbols and paintings in a symmetrically even tenor play an important and dynamic role in the Vajra-yana. Here the meditator can retire day and night and carry out his oblations and prostrations within the three-fold vehicle of body, mind and speech.

Twice per day, one can have an interview with Akong on one's particular path or sadhana. However, Akong related to me that a proportion of the people attending the centre came for psychological help. This ranged from drug addicts to those complaining of mental disorders. Nevertheless, do not get me wrong, Samye-Ling is *not* a mental hospital. The people who have visited the Centre in the past with mental problems are a strict minority.

Those 'taking Refuge' can, after careful consideration, request Akong to carry out the necessary ceremonial and go on retreat for three or more days. One of Samye-Ling's strong points is that it has several huts lying on the outskirts of the grounds which provide an ideal setting for reflective study, meditation and devotion. The meals of the day can be arranged to be brought to the hut so as communication and involvement with people is reduced to an absolute minimum.

The Library, sometimes a focal point for discussions with visitors, contains some 2000 books on religion, philosophy, psychology, science, nature study and, would you believe, *Custer's Last Stand*! It has one of those ageing paper smells, not offensive, but which stimulates one's mind and thoughts. Periodicals abound; there are literally hundreds of them ranging from the ubiquitous *Middle Way* to the scholarly *Buddhist Quarterly*, the journal of the British Mahabodhi Society. Because the Centre attracts people from all over Europe, the Library also has a limited number of Buddhist and non-Buddhist books and dictionaries in foreign languages.

Personal Reflections

Samye-Ling to me is one of the most ideally situated Dharma centres in Britain. Being so secluded and peaceful it makes for a deepening of inner peace and makes meditation that little bit easier and enjoyable. The vibratory level of a spiritual community such as Samye-Ling is founded on the people in it, just as a seventy-man orchestra will perform to the limits of excellence depending on the virtuosity of the individual instrumentalist.

The rising bell sounds at 5.45 a.m. every morning summoning the devout to Puja. For obvious reasons not everyone attends Puja which lasts for an hour but is very interesting to partake in. After having a quick wash in the toilet and shower-room, which is nearly always kept spotless, it's off downstairs for the first meal of the day. In the dining-room, which has lovely hand-carved chairs and tables along with various paintings of Bodhisattvas and woodblock prints, one serves oneself with a bowl of porridge or, in the summer, muesli. This is followed by toast and a cup of tea. The Centre is totally vegetarian, and no meat in any form is eaten. Buddhists refrain from meat-eating, seeing in this an expression for their reverence for life, from the smallest insect to the largest mammal. If we are thoroughly to root out hatred and unwholesome thoughts and actions from our minds and bodies, then this is one of the disciplines which leads to the antithetical states of compassion, kindness and moderation in eating.

The first group meditation of the day commences at 8.00 a.m. Again the resounding humming tones of the communal gong summon the meditators to the Shrine Room. At the entrance to the room lies a conglomeration of variously shaped cushions, a must for the meditator embarking on an hour-long session. Here are gathered together Buddhists meditators of all schools, although the majority at any one time are following the Vajrayanic path. After lighting incense and offering it to the Shrine, the meditation leader strikes the gong thrice to begin the meditation. Each meditation session culminates with three long sonorous reverberations of the gong, sometimes to the relief of the meditators. To sit in the full or half lotus for an hour can be an accomplishment in itself, never mind the concentrative effort involved.

Between 9.00 a.m. and 12.30 p.m. one is either engaged in private study, meditation or an interview with Akong is arranged. Another feature of Samye-Ling, although not wholly characteristic of the Centre itself, is the work schedule. The work is allocated either by Akong himself or a long-term resident and is basically twofold – inside or outside the main building. The women carry out the domestic duties of cleaning and dusting, hoovering, washing, tidying-up and, most important of all, the preparation of the meals. The men are usually engaged in building repairs (in a relatively old building as this there is generally a list of odd-jobs needing done), feeding the chickens, cows and pets, etc., chopping wood and doing gardening.

Apart from routine chores there are various craft facilities at the Centre. Amongst the many crafts are weaving, wood-block printing and pottery. These are invariably sold in the Centre's shop which also sells articles such as books, clothes, beads, Buddharupas, incense, candles and lots more. Shera-palden Beru is the chief artist and in fact is stated to be the foremost authority on Tibetan thankas outside of Tibet. This has been further ratified by the fact that he was invited by the King of Sikkim to produce some paintings to be hung in the Royal Palace at Gangtok before his coming to the West.

The gong again is struck at 12.30 p.m. for lunch. Again it's self-service, beginning with the main course, usually comprising the inevitable brown rice, sometimes mixed with buck-wheat, vegetable pie, salad and sometimes daily produce. For seconds it's fruit pie or flan, sometimes yogurt and raw fruit, which is finally 'washed down' with a hot cup of tea.

Another rule adhered to at the Centre, and again I must reiterate that it is not totally exclusive to Samye-Ling, is that of abstention from smoking. Apart from there being no ashtrays provided for cigarette smokers, the fire hazard is the obvious reason for this rule being implemented. On a more spiritual level, I feel that it is simply another attachment which brings its accompanying burden and suffering. No alcohol or drugs of any kind (excluding those prescribed by a doctor) are permitted in Samye-Ling. The reasons for this are obvious.

Between 1.30 and 5.00 another work period takes place. This is another ideal time to make more acquaintances and friends and to discuss all those spiritual topics which tends to keep one centred on one's path. At 5.00 p.m. another hour-long meditation session ensues before soup at 6.30. The 'soup' is usually an urnful of the vegetable left-overs from lunch mixed with herbs. A community like Samye-Ling, which literally subsists on its own resources, must economize where possible. The 'soup meal' is one of those areas. Anyhow, the soup I've tasted at the Centre has always been first class.

Evening Puja takes place at 8.00 p.m. which usually ends in meditation. After 10.00 the Shrine Room is open to anyone in which to meditate, even all through the night if one wishes so.

The Gyalwa Karmapa's visit in 1975

From time to time the Centre is blessed with the appearance of eminent Buddhist monks, scholars, and teachers. In 1975 His Holiness the Gyalwa Karmapa, the sixteenth, visited Britain after a successful mission to America. He arrived at Prestwick Airport along with a retinue of twelve Lamas and was greeted by Akong Tarap Rimpoche.

After formal greetings and salutations the assembly drove off to Samye-Ling. At the Centre, which had been for weeks a hive of activity in the preparations for the visit, many people congregated in anticipation of this great personage. On his arrival he immediately retired to the Shrine Room to meditate and give blessings. The following day, which happened to be a New Moon day, His Holiness performed the Vajra Crown Ceremony and a Milarepa initiation to a packed 'audience'. As a parallel to this, he later performed the Karma Pakshi and Manjushri initiations. As part of his service and upholding of his Bodhisattva Vow, His Holiness instructed many people in meditation and also conducted individual interviews for those having problems with their sadhana.

A unique event took place on the third week of His Holiness's visit. This was the ordination of ten Westerners into the Buddhist Sangha. A sure sign that the reality of a Western monastic community is with us; I sincerely hope for many years to come.

From Samye-Ling His Holiness travelled to Kham Tibetan house, Saffron Walden, where he conducted the Crown Ceremony and gave initiations. From here it was off to London for more initiations and ceremonies, along with a visit to Westminster Abbey.*

*For the record: the Gyalwa Karmapa returned to Britain in the winter of 1977 to 1978 and undertook an intensive programme of ceremonies and

One ending this section, I would like to congratulate Akong Tarap Rimpoche for the amount of hard work and creativity which he is daily undertaking in the advancement of Tibetan Buddhism in Britain. When one realizes that Samye-Ling is the 'parent centre' of over thirty Tibetan Centres in Europe, one begins to understand the enormity and pre-eminence of this beautifully colourful gompa in the heart of southern Scotland. The next time you have a week to spare, why not take a trip to Samye-Ling? I'm convinced that you will come away with intentions for your next visit.

Kham Tibetan House

Kham Tibetan House was officially opened on Saturday, 10 November, 1973 by HRH Crown Prince Tenzing Namgyal of Sikkim.†

Kham House is basically a retreat for the pilgrim or adept who wishes to retire from the hubbub and turmoil of the city, to purify both mind and body in tranquil surroundings. The house is located about half a mile from the small village of Ashdon, in the heart of Essex, near Saffron Walden.

The existence of such an institution is largely due to the untiring effort of Lama Chime Rimpoche, one of the many Lamas to have come out of Tibet in recent years. But I must not forget the small band of students who have stuck with Chime through thick and thin, in his endeavours to have such a centre established. It became apparent after the formation of

---

initiations. He was accompanied on his trip by such high-ranking teachers as Jamgon Kangtrul Gyaltso, himself a high-ranking teacher, and Khenpo Tsultim Gyaltso, a master of Mahamudra and the Six Doctrines, now resident at Dhagpo Kagyu Ling at Dordogne, France.

His holiness visited and, subsequently, lectured at Karma Cho-Ling, the Buddhist Society and other centres in London. He also lectured at Kham House, Marpa Institute and Samye-Ling prior to his return to the East on 3 January 1978.

†More of the opening ceremony will be outlined later in this section.

Samye-Ling, that one Tibetan centre was totally inadequate to fulfil the requirements of a growing number of people interested in Tibetan Buddhism.

The centre is dedicated to the upholding of the teachings of the Kagyudpa School of Tibetan Buddhism, although anybody, no matter what his creed, will find tolerance and respect for his beliefs. Like Samye-Ling, Kham House has HH the Gyalwa Karmapa (Dhusum Khenpa) as its Spiritual Patron, the living presence carrying on the mystical oral teachings transmitted from the Divine Guru of the school, the celestial Buddha Dorje Chang.

Lama Chime Rimpoche has been in Britain for some twelve years now and has partaken in most of the important Buddhist events that have occurred over the years. Between 1966 and 1970 a new generation of Truth-seekers appeared on the scene, and it just so happened that an influx of Tibetan Lamas and Tulkus appeared – a coincidence! These new would-be Buddhists sought out not only the Tibetans but Zen Roshis and Thai monks, people who not only intellectually instructed their pupils but exemplified the Enlightenment principle by their mere presence. Chime, seeing the enthusiasm of British people in general, felt a centre in England would prove beneficial, especially if it were near London. However, Chime went out to the States to feel the atmosphere there just in case; he also looked briefly at Canada but terminated his tour, even although he had arranged to lecture at Yale University.

The trip to the States and Canada provided Chime with the chance to survey the spiritual quality of the people, as well as to provide money for his heart-felt wish. On his arrival back in England he decided to return to India – to his teachers, and to his uncle Dilgo Khentse Rimpoche. During his stay he spent some time with the Gyalwa Karmapa in Sikkim. The recurrent theme expressed by all his teachers was that he should return to England, to teach the Westerners and hopefully, to establish a solid foundation on which to build a refuge for the Kagyu School of Tibetan Buddhism.

When back in England Chime, along with a small group of

faithful students, embarked upon a search for some property to establish the centre. As Scotland already had Samye-Ling, they looked towards Wales in the hope that prices would be rather less extortionate – but they weren't. During 1972 Britain was undergoing a property boom, where prices were rocketing in the face of raging inflation.

However, some friends later informed Chime of a small property going in Ashdon which would suit his requirements down to the ground. It was clean, isolated, yet near enough to London, would require little decorating and, what's most important, had a large expanse at the rear in which a vegetable plot could be cultivated. The house, which had previously been a children's home, immediately impressed Chime, whereupon the sole thing left to do was to raise the funds to purchase it.

In 1972, a year before he founded Kham House, Chime visited the British Museum to study various relics on show. During his visit, he was asked by the museum official why he was attending the museum and enquired of his business in England. When the authorities realized that he was in fact a fully incarnate Lama, they immediately asked him if he would like a job in the Oriental Manuscript Department. After his visit to the department and realizing that there was a complete set of the *Kanjur and Tanjur*, the sacred texts of the Kagyu and Nyingma schools respectively, Chime accepted their proposals and hence found himself employed. But if he was to succeed in his venture, he found it increasingly valuable that to live and work as does a Westerner, and even to get married, would greatly improve relations between him and his students.

The house was bought in 1972 primarily from funds donated by various friends of Chime, all of whom had some ties with Buddhism. From the outset, Chime made it quite clear that if the house was to run smoothly and economically he would have to have the final say on pressing decisions. On the face of it, it sounds all very totalitarian but, in fact, if a person had more knowledge and 'know-how' about the running of a community such as Kham, it was then a simple matter of logic that he or she should authorize the affairs.

All those who stayed or had close associations with Kham during the first year will know what I mean. Anyhow, wasn't Chime the Abbot of Benchen monastery prior to his flight from Tibet? Actually this gives one a discreet insight into the theocratic policy of Tibetan life.

In autumn 1972 Chime decided to marry, the girl in question being Celia Jane Pertwee, who had done a secretarial job in London. By this time he was 'out of the robe' but technically still a Lama. Kham House was purchased, and the following week-end a handful of people moved in, with the first guests arriving mid-week. The actual condition of the house was luckily first-class with little or no decorating needed, so the promptness at which the arrival of the first visitors to the house was executed tended to catch the haughty owners unawares.

The first year was a year of cautious reticence, a year in which the new community was all too aware of its nondescript image, an image which I must assert was totally in the eye of the beholder. It could be likened to the sudden appearance of the radiantly white swan amongst a gaggle of geese. So, confrontation was avoided at all costs with the villagers and, if anything, an attitude of respect towards them was exercised. It was a year where the handful of helpers wanted prayer flags, multi-coloured rooms and ecclesiastical accoutrements. But all this was refuted by Chime on the grounds that it led to over-indulgence in the 'Tibetan trip' rather than the unbiased transplantation of Tibetan Buddhism in English soil.

Many of Kham's first visitors throughout the year came with various idiosyncratic expectations about the house, 'the scene', the teachings and the general atmosphere that pervaded the running of such an establishment. And through time an image was conceived, not to its detriment, but to the peaceful and humble surroundings and the punctilious attitude of the people who made the house tick.

Probably the most irreverent episode which materialized during that year was the financial arrangements and relationships which Chime had with his pupils. Here there existed the contrary situation where Frank McAllen and Keith Loveard, two of Chime's closest followers, sat and meditated or did puja, whilst the 'guru' Chime went to work. However, this was not, I may add, a conscious contrivance but a spontaneous event which occurred by itself. On the other hand, it showed the compassion with which Chime employed in his dealings with people in general.

In July 1973, Celia, Chime's wife, had a baby daughter called Pema. The baby was born in Cambridge and was not only a new addition to the family, but a new resident to Kham House. During this time Chime and his wife were living in the small flat at the top of the house. Like all children Pema cried, talked, squealed and made all the other multifarious sounds issuing from a small child. This in turn led to a daily surveillance on baby Pema and an all-out effort in keeping her quiet.

The Shrine Room at this time was beginning to take shape. A small linen-covered table, puja bowls, incense and the Karmapas's photograph provided the focal point in the room – nothing fancy, just humble and unostentatious. The austerity was slightly alleviated by the arrival of several Thanka paintings and only latterly did they procure their first rupa – a brass image of Tara*, donated by a visitor.

During Easter 1973, Chime held a week-end Seminar on the Four Foundations and the Six Doctrines of Naropa at Kham House, which was attended by a zealous and sincere assemblage. After this he was invited out to India and Nepal to act as Tibetan Adviser on the BBC film documentary called *The Roaring Silence*. The film was basically outlining the emergence of Tibetan Buddhism in India after the invasion of Tibet by China. Although Chime never took part in the film, his experience, knowledge and standing on Tibetan Buddhism were invaluable. Although his absence went without considering regret, it soon became obvious that his physical presence was as a battery of inspiration and, on his eventual return, glad tidings were expressive of all the community at the house.

*A female deity used in Vajrayanic meditational practices.

The Grand Opening

The Grand Opening of Kham Tibetan House took place in November of 1973, and had the added boon of being the official 'housewarming'. All and sundry were invited along with many of the locals of Ashdon and surrounding districts. An artful piece of opportunism by Chime was to invite the chief of police to the opening as a means of showing that the house was 'straight'. This event had delightful karmic repercussions in the inclusion by the police chief in inviting two constables to operate point duty.

In his opening address, Chime showed his appreciation of the fact that many people had journeyed from afar to the opening of the house, especially from Switzerland, Denmark and France. He included also those close friends who had negated their own personal idiosyncracies in their wish to have Kham House established, some of those being Celia, Chime's wife, Keith and Joanna Loveard and Frank McAllen. Chime reflected on the hardships accrued by him during his flight from the Communists:

'And I for one was admitted to hospital seriously ill. When my health had slightly improved I made my way to Sikkim and stayed in a village in the mountains and here the people cared for me and gave me a cup of milk every day until I gained my strength. I was then able to work for my people and eventually to come to the West to uphold Tibetan religion and culture for the benefit of all people.'

After a brief oration of gratitude to Prince Tenzing Namgyal and his father the King, who had instigated a programme of help and assistance to thousands of Tibetan refugees, Chime then welcomed the Prince to declare Kham House open.

The Prince began his speech by honouring Lama Dhime Rimpoche for the strength of purpose he had displayed in the establishing of a Tibetan centre in England. He then proceeded to elaborate on the part played by religion in such endeavours:

'Thus religion enables us to drive this satisfaction from the mind by teaching us to control our minds so that we may be able to prevent evil thoughts which so often result in evil actions, leading to evil effects on the mind.'

Remaining on the same basic theme played by religion, the Prince continued by explaining the interest of Westerners in Buddhism:

'Examples of [Eastern religious thought] can be seen by the increasing amount of people travelling from the West to the East on pilgrimage and at home by the number of books being read coupled with the growing numbers of peoples studying and practising meditation and other aspects of Buddhism.'

Prince Tenzing continued by highlighting the exchange of thought and cultures of East–West democracies which culminated in the Dalai Lama's visit to England that same year. Also, the numbers of Tibetans who had come over from India in recent years had grown and the Kham House would provide 'a sanctuary for re-orientating themselves to the heritage that is theirs'.

The large collection of Tibetan manuscripts housed at the Prince's Institution in Sikkim, he said, were in the process of being micro-filmed, and would be made available for Europeans in the future. The Prince ended his speech by specifying the role played by Kham Tibetan House in the propagation of Tibetan teachings in England:

'It also serves to preserve the tradition, culture, and the way of life of the Tibetan people. It is a centre of learning where there is a free exchange of ideas and their development. With all this, I feel that the future is a secure and bright one and this House will be a great benefit to all who come here.'

He then declared Kham Tibetan House open.*

As a *dénouement* to the opening of the House, Chime successfully had the first 300 *Vajra* journals published, the official 'voice' of Kham Tibetan House.

The year 1974 was a year of visitors and the rudiments of the first Western Tibetan Sangha in Britain. During the year, the House welcomed – Geshe Rabten, presently the Abbot of Rikon Monastery in Zurich. In July, the Very Venerable

*The Prince was at this time studying at Cambridge University.

Lama Kalu Rimpoche visited the House during his tour of Britain. Kalu Rimpoche who was the Meditation Teacher at Palpung Monastery in eastern Tibet, is presently involved in directing a three-year retreat for Westerners in France. Whilst at Kham he gave Chenrezig initiations. And lastly, in December, as part of his British tour, His Holiness the Gyalwa Karmapa visited the House for a few days.

Whilst the Karmapa was in Britain he carried out ordinations of Westerners into the Sangha. Some of the ten who took the robe that day were associated with Kham House. They went through the usual procedures of shaven heads, the acceptance of the maroon and ochre robes and the embracing of the gelung* vows. In the evening His Holiness performed the Vajra Crown Ceremony followed by a Chenresig Initiation – and six Westerners found themselves transformed into the living Sangha.

In 1975, the House took on a different and inspiring appearance, which manifested in the impressibility the monks instilled in the visitors to the House. Chime encouraged the monks in Tibetan and Dharma studies which, on the face of it, was proving successful. However, this happy and congenial state of affairs came to an abrupt end – basically for two reasons, one spiritual, the other financial. From the point of precedence it was obvious that the latter reason was of more consequence to Kham House. To begin with the House was too noisy for the monks to study and meditate in peace and serenity, a prerequisite for a monkish life. There were also many niggling reasons appertaining to their vows which made this life impossible, for example, a monk must not in any circumstances be found alone with a woman in the same room – *with door closed!* Anyway, Kham House was a meditation centre-cum-retreat, not a monastery.

Secondly, an institution like Kham, which relied totally on visitors fees for its upkeep, was slowly going into the red. After all, here were six monks taking up beds which could have been more profitably utilized by visitors. So the house

*This is the Tibetan appellation for the Pali term Bhikkhu.

was carrying monks, financially worse off and an air of incredulity descended on the community. By the end of that summer the monks felt a trifle disillusioned with no one to model themselves on and, suddenly, it was just a handful of people who had previously had close ties with the House wearing different clothes. The Vinaya Rules had by now become such a burden that Chime felt that the honourable way out was to disband the group – nevertheless, it was an interesting experience for all who took part and I'm convinced that many lessons were learned.

Kham House, from the outset, was and still is very much a meditation centre. Chime has always advised against study at Kham and it was under these prevailing circumstances that a friend of Chime's offered a property at Bury St Edmunds which later became a study centre called the Marpa Institute, registered under the Dharma Trust.*

In 1976, Frank McAllen took over as Secretary at Kham and has related to me how the growth of visitors to the House, especially from America and Holland, were warmly welcomed. During this time the number of people doing the Four Foundations† was very much in evidence. A visitor at the House in February of 1976 was Dilgo Khentse Rimpoche, who is the spiritual adviser to the Royal Family of Bhutan. Carrying the Nyingma tradition of Tibetan Buddhism, he is recognized as a Terton,‡ and it was he who opened the Marpa Institute the same month.

*The Dharma Trust was created by Lama Chime Rimpoche and provides all the financial and spiritual requirements of the two centres of Marpa Institute and the newly formed Karma-Choling in London. To save the reader from confusion, there also exists the Kagyu Trust, which is a totally different entity from the Dharma Trust. The Kagyu Trust was established by HH the Gyalwa Karmapa principally to monitor the Tibetan teachings in the West. It has as its Chairman, John Maxwell.

†The Four Foundations are the fundamental spiritual disciplines exercised by those leading and following the doctrines of the four major schools of Tibetan Buddhism.

‡A Terton is one who has discovered a hidden teaching which relates back to Padmasambhava himself.

At present Kham House is run by a staff of about three, although this figure fluctuates according to circumstances. Visitors are not allowed to bring alcohol or drugs into the house. Only sincere pilgrims are requested and, in its relatively short history, it has not had occasion to turn anybody away or to refuse entrance. All Buddhists living at the house, no matter the length of residence, are obliged to live according to the Precepts, and an atmosphere of quietness is demanded. For those who require a full and intensive residence one could participate in the following programme:

Rising Bell   6.30 a.m.
Tara Puja   7.00 a.m.
Silent meditation 11.00 a.m.
Silent meditation 5.00 p.m.
Chenresig Puja   8.00 p.m.

Running concurrent to this is one's Foundation practice which would be done in the Practice Room opposite the Shrine Room between the above hours.

If a person is spiritually receptive enough, with a good basic knowledge of Buddhism, he can, if he so wishes, go for Refuge. This would take the form of an individual interview with Chime in the Shrine Room, which in a sense provides the new adept with a special link with him. One is then given a Tibetan name and possibly a simple meditation technique, but in some cases one will begin the Four Foundations if one has some fundamental knowledge of what this involves.

Kham Tibetan House provides the serious student of Buddhism with all the necessary surroundings and 'props' in which to advance in his Sadhana. As with most Buddhist centres up and down the country, all the food served is vegetarian and, I must confess, absolutely beautiful. One will always be treated with respect and kindness at Kham as I found out when I visited it with my wife and son.

The wish-fulfilling gem and the jewel in the lotus, the Four Foundations

As mentioned earlier, the inception of Vajrayanic practice is the Four Foundations, the grounding for all advanced practice. All Vajrayanic practices begin with initiations as prescribed by the 'root-lama', who provides the 'wish-fulfilling gem' of the teaching. Mahamudra meditation, as associated with the Kagyu school, empowers us to unify body, speech and mind in such a way that the eventual results lead to the development of Bodhi and the awakening of the great compassion (Mahakaruna) within us as exemplified by the various Bodhisattvas of the Mahayana tradition.

1 The great prostrations

As with the following foundations, each one employs the interaction of body, speech and mind to negate the ego, transmute our confusion and the clear perception of undifferentiated Sunyata. The main theme running through this practice is the ultimate surrender of our egotistic attachments to the 'I' and the removal of all psycho-physical hindrances standing in our attainment of Buddhahood.

One performs the three-fold practice of prostration, an offering of our body to the Triratna, the recitation of the Threefold Refuge and the mental visualization of the Kagyu lineage – 100,000 times. In this practice great devotion is discovered within us which leads to an opening up to and, transcendental mergence with, the lineage which becomes dissolved within our hearts.

2 Purification by meditating on Vajrasattva (Dorje Sempa)

Vajrasattva or the Adamantine Being represents the pure, illimitable pristine purity of mind. Here the adept visualize the immaculate form of Vajrasattva whilst reciting the 'Hundred Syllable Mantra' of Vajrasattva. This Foundation has the effect of destroying the mental impurities such as greed, hatred and delusion and the subsequent evolution of the contrasting qualities of charity, benevolence and enlightenment. The power of Dorje Sempa purges one of the obscurations and reveals the radiant light of our void-nature.

3   *The Mandala offering*

In this Foundation the adept makes an offering of a Mandala in the form of the material universe consisting of all the galaxies, solar systems and nebulae to the lineage of lamas, Bodhisattvas, etc. This meditation has the effect of accumulating merit which, being aware of the potential attachment to the good Karma issuing from this need, the adept immediately returns the wholesome effects of his practice for the benefit of all sentient beings. Again compassion and ego-negation is aimed at and, the turning away from thoughts of 'self' to thoughts of others.

4   *The practice of Guru Yoga*

This is probably the most important and consequently the most difficult of the Foundations. Here the adept must be prepared to unite his mind with that of the lama's to the point where all sounds heard is the speech of the lama. Also, all visual appearances become the form of the lama and all discursive thought and ideas become the mind of the lama.

To acquire this state of consciousness requires of us utter faith and devotion to the lineage invoking their blessings which accentuates the confluence of our mind to that of the lama's. However, the difficulties we may encounter throughout this Foundation will be minimal if the previous three are performed with sincerity, veneration and heedfulness.*

---

*For further reading on the theoretical and practical aspects of Vajrayanic practices, the writer strongly advises John Blofeld's *Way of Power*, Allen and Unwin, London 1970; Dutton, New York 1970 (as *The Tantric Mysticism of Tibet*).

The Sacred Ceremony of the Vajra Crown

Two thousand years after my death,
The teachings will come to the land of the red-faced people,
Who will be enabled to accept the Dharma through the
    power of Avalokitesvara.
When the teachings become corrupted in that country,
The lion-voiced Bodhisattva called Karmapa will come.
The power he attains in samadhi he will transmit to benefit
    sentient beings.
By either seeing, hearing, touching or thinking of him
They will be brought to happiness.

SAKYAMUNI BUDDHA in the *Samadhiraja Sutra*

The Gyalwa Karmapa is the ideal personification of Wisdom
and Compassion, the Enlightenment principle in human form.
Being masters of Tantra, all the Karmapas from the first,
Dusum Khyenpa (AD 1110–93) to the present Rangjung Rigpe
Dorge (AD 1927) have bestowed limitless blessings on
mankind, such is their love of sentient beings.

The Vajra Crown Ceremony is an event which subsequent
Karmapas have performed as a vehicle for the distribution of
blessings to both Sangha and laity alike. The original Vajra
Crown was first worn by the Fifth Karmapa, Deshin Shegpa
(1384–1415). Whilst in China at the invitation of the emperor
Ch'eng Tus, the emperor was overawed at the holiness of the
Karmapa and eventually became an ardent disciple. However,
during a ceremony being conducted by HH Deshin Shegpa,
the new disciple saw an invisible crown hovering above the
Karmapa's head. To procure the lasting effect of this vision,
the emperor set about having an exact replica made as an object
of veneration.

Legend has it that the transcendental form of the Vajra
Crown was constructed from the hairs of a hundred thousand
Dakinis. To those of inestimable spiritual power the invisible
crown becomes manifest, an assurance to the percipient of his
attainment to the highest bliss in his lifetime. Although the

actual physical Vajra Crown continues as a symbol, one must become totally conscious of its immaterial counterpart.

The ceremony

His Holiness the Gyalwa Karmapa sits on an elevated throne. He is wearing a crown other than the Vajra Crown, sometimes the meditation hat of Gampopa, sometimes a red conical hat. He is surrounded by his monks and, beyond them, the audience. The monks begin to chant. In what they chant and do, they, represent the entire gathering in a prolonged request that Karmapa assume his transcendental form of Avalokitesvara, the Bodhisattva of compassion.

First addressing Karmapa as Dusum Khyenpa, the manifestation of Avalokitesvara, they invoke the presence of the Karmapa lineage. Then, as a metal disc with rice on it, a symbolic offering is made of the entire universe as a mandala. Then the action of the invocation takes the form of the traditional seven-fold service. First is a prostration expressing devotion to Karmapa – Avalokitesvara. Offerings are made symbolizing the body, speech and mind of the supplicants. Acknowledgement of misguidedness and imperfection is made with a sense of surrendering to the higher wisdom becoming present. There is praise and adoration of the Buddha-activity of Avalokitesvara. A request is made that Karmapa-Avalokitesvara turn the wheel of the Dharma, making the teachings manifest. There is a further request that he remain in the world and not die. The seven-fold service is ended by dedicating the benefits of the activities of the participants to all sentient beings.

In response to the supplication, His Holiness removes his hat. At this time he is opening himself and preparing to enter wholly and completely into his manifestation as Avalokitesvara, totally awakened and radiating the energy of compassion. In relation to the meeting of minds which can take place in this ceremony, the audience cannot remain passive. Ideally, every member of the audience will have made a gift. Having made a gift and having participated in the surrendering and opening of the invocation and seven-fold service, the participant has fully prepared the ground for a process of free exchange. As His Holiness places the Vajra Crown on his head and repeats the 'Om Mani Padme Hum' mantra, the audience should be fully attentive to him and permit its awareness to merge with his. The placing of the hat and the telling of one hundred 'mani' mantras completes the link with his transcendental aspect and with the audience. His Holiness removes the Vajra Crown and the ceremony is ended by the chanting of the monks, dedicating the benefits arising from the ceremony to all sentient beings and asking for long life for His Holiness.

There is absolutely no compulsory payment required for admission to the Sacred Ceremony of the Vajra Crown. However, it should be clearly understood that a voluntary offering could make a significant contribution to your own ability to open to, and receive the transmission of Karmapa-Avalokitesvara. Giving something of value expresses surrender of one's possessive or materialistic outlook, of one's clinging and attachment. Through the seven-fold service, giving becomes surrender, surrender becomes devotion and devotion a medium of communication. One's gift, then, may be the step which initiates the link between oneself and the lineage.

> I, Tilopa, smile and say: ...
> Look with unswerving faith and love
> At the Jewel of a Guru.

The Manjushri Institute

The Institute, which has had a relatively short history (approximately one year at the time of writing this book), is, I feel, going to be probably the most momentous and invaluable centre for Dharma study and dissemination, not only in Britain but in the whole of Europe. And I say this because the centre not only teaches Buddhism – it lives it! If you only want to generalize, proselytize or analyse Buddhism, well, my only

E

answer to that is – don't go to Manjushri. On the surface, this seems negative and I personally don't indulge in negativity; it's not my nature. But when describing the motivation of the residents, Sangha members and Institute Directors, one gets the feeling that the Dharma is being revitalized and it would seem to me that they are succeeding beyond their own wildest dreams.

Being a Tibetan centre, it naturally concentrates on Tibetan religion, culture and traditions and is adequately served by a handful of Lamas, some of whom are the most enlightened men walking this earth today. But this is what gives Manjushri its especial flavour – the Sangha. Apart from the Tibetans and Nepalese, the Institute has striven to organize and promote, the first lasting Western Sangha of Tibetan Buddhism, totally comprised of men and women from the Occident. Added to this is the Institute's innovatory College of Tibetan Buddhist Studies. The College will be run, hand in hand, with the community, which, when finally established will be the first 'Tibetan College' in Britain, and possibly in Europe. However, more of that later.

Before I continue, I would like to make clear to the reader that, although the Institute is dedicated to the teachings and Dharma as found in the Gelugpa school of Tibetan Buddhism, it cordially welcomes everybody, Buddhist or not, to come and sample the 'goods'. The Institute is always running introductory courses on basic Lam.rim,* so that even the novice, after a little practice, will find and even be inspired enough, to return and take further instruction and possibly a course at the College.

The Institute

Conishead Priory and its sixty-nine acres of fields, woodlands, foreshore, gardens and buildings, make up a magnificent historic tableau dating back to the twelfth century. It appears

---

*A Tibetan term to denote the 'Gradual Path to Enlightenment' found in the Gelugpa school of Tibetan Bhuddism, and taught at the Institute.

augural that the Priory, which was once inhabited by Augustinian monks, has now more than seven centuries later, become the abode of a thriving Buddhist community of monks, nuns and laymen.

The Priory was founded during the reign of King Henry II by one Gamel de Pennington. During the twelfth century, the Priory, which housed paupers and lepers cared for by the monks, later maintained a school. The Priory school would generally attract a fair number of local boys, the brightest being inducted into the Order of St Augustine as a matter of course. This tradition endured for three centuries, up until 1536, and the coming into power of King Henry VIII. Henry, who was for the most part anti-monastic, broke ties with Rome and introduced a period of so-called religious reform, dissolving monasteries and subduing Catholicism.

After the dissolution of the Priory, the complete estate changed hands for three centuries when, in the middle of the eighteenth century, the Priory underwent substantial repair under the ownership of Thomas Richmond Braddyll. His extensive re-design and architectural 'adornments' left him with an impossible financial burden which pressed him to sell the property. It was duly bought by a Scotsman, Mr Henry Askew, who later sold it in 1878 to a Scottish syndicate, who seeing the many natural resources of the surrounding countryside, turned it into a hydropathic health resort and sauna. In 1929, however, the property was sold again, this time to the Durham Miners Welfare Committee, which they utilized as a convalescent home for ageing miners and also for those suffering from diseases and ailments contracted in the mines.

During the war years, the Priory was used as an Emergency Hospital and in 1972 was once more put up for sale, where the estate was sub-divided into lots. The Priory itself, plus seventy acres, were bought; but the building was unfortunately uninhabited and pitifully left to the elements, where dampness and dry-rot penetrated much of the interior. Because of this, decay set in, destroying some beautiful ornamental plasterwork, with fungus growing rife.

Four years later, in early 1976, the Priory was again up for sale, and it was during those months that contact was made with the then present owner, a Wigan building contractor. Contracts were exchanged by the two parties and, by late spring, the Priory was again in safe hands – with a major renovation project put into action.

The Manjushri Institute, has, to my knowledge, existed in name and form for a couple of years. This has been the initial work of two men, Harvey Horrocks, the present Director of the Institute, and Peter Kedge. Both had previously been studying under the eminent Tibetan Lama Thubten Yeshe in Nepal. When both arrived back in Britain, they decided to try to establish a centre with Harvey continuing the work from his home in London. But this proved quite inadequate and luckily enough was offered accommodation and office facilities at the Mahayana Buddhist Temple in Bromley. The Temple was an energetic Tibetan centre run by two nuns Ani Tsultim Zangmo and Ani Wongchuk Palmo, which had previously been their home before their ordinations into the Tibetan Sangha three years beforehand. Together, Harvey and Peter Kedge staged a week-long seminar at Holloway College, London; after it Harvey took up residence at the Temple and Peter returned to Nepal.

In the latter half of 1975, the search proceeded for a permanent centre. But even at this time, the Manjushri Institute, had already been arranging seminars and courses which were conducted by such exalted figures as Ven. Geshe Rabten, Ven. Lama Thubten Yeshe, Ven. Lama Thubten Zopa Rimpoche and Geshe Tsultim Gyeltsen. Throughout the beginnings of the Institute, their name, the work they were doing and the seriousness of Dharma study being undertaken, became widely known.

During the late spring and early summer of 1976, the search was stepped up, with another active associate of the Institute Dennis Heslop taking on the task of surveying the many properties throughout Wales and the Lake District. These two areas were surveyed as being in conformity to the suggestions of the Lama's as being conducive to the advancement of meditation and Dharma study.

In February 1976, the Institute published a newsletter outlining the present situation, and had a circulation of about 400 people, both in Britain and abroad. Meetings were also being held at the Buddhist Society's headquarters at Eccleston Square, in the form of discourses by the Geshe Tsultim Gyeltsen. The Sangha Trust at Haverstock Hill in London, also provided facilities for weekly puja/meditation sessions. The newsletter also reported on the projected teaching programme at the International Mahayana Institute, a Nepalese Gompa housing forty Western Sangha members (monks and nuns), and the news of courses being held throughout Europe.

A month later, Conishead Priory, which had previously been on the 'surveillance' list, was inspected. Although dry-rot permeated much of the buildings, the beauty of the Priory along with the peaceful rustic surroundings, made it a most ideal setting for self-recollection and awareness. Whilst at the Priory, Harvey Horrocks and his working party, took photographs and details of the work required, and what is most important, the anticipated costs involved. Two weeks later at a course run at Pangbourne College, near Reading, by the Ven. Geshe Rabten,* a meeting was held whereby Harvey described the condition of the Priory, the expenses involved and the sheer volume of hard work needing done to get the Manjushri Institute established in its own home. After considerable debate, the 'audience' showed mixed feelings about the project and particularly the financial side.

In May it was decided to go ahead with serious investigation into the feasibility of buying the Priory. The decision to actually go ahead and purchase was not made until much later, when it was found that the Priory would be suitable. After balancing the books, as it were, an offer was made to the owner, which he rejected outright. Needless to say the project came to a

*Ven. Geshe Rabten is the present Abbot of the Tibetan Monastic Institute at Rikon, Switzerland.

grinding halt. A meeting was immediately held where it was agreed to submit a higher offer subject to contract, but formal negotiations were not entered into until it was fairly clear that an appeal would raise enough capital for a deposit.

Four weeks later, an appeal was launched to raise the money for the deposit on the Priory. The Institute circulated an appeal booklet outlining the situation and, what I felt most novel, a list of ways in which one could provide support. This ranged from purchasing a self-contained flat within the Priory, to simply making an interest-free loan (minimum £500), to buying an accommodation package deal (6 weeks at the Priory for £25), or to subscribing to the Institute's newsletter.

The question was asked, that if we in the West were that desirous of leading a life in the Dharma, then to what extent should we sacrifice our possessions in such a circumstance. Anyway, exactly what was the Manjushri Institute about? This was summed up by Lama Thubten Yeshe:

The purpose of the Institute is, I think, to provide conditions for the complete practice of the Graduated Path as experienced by Atisa and Lama Tsongkapa. My point of view is that this is both important and worthwhile. To make possible the complete path, from beginning to end, Enlightenment is so worthwhile. If the centre becomes a mixture – a kind of samsaric trip, then what is the purpose of putting energy into it? I think that we don't need that. Actually the real purpose of the centre, is that we are serving. We are so fortunate to have made contact with the Mahayana Dharma of Lord Buddha, and are trying to share our experience. Only for that purpose is the centre established.

By August, the deposit had been accumulated and paid, an advanced working party moved in immediately to carry out initial reclamation duties. Ten days later, due to the tenacity and strength of commitment of the advanced party, the Institute publicly offered their first meditation course. The twenty-three-day course, which was attended by no less than seventy people, was conducted by the lamas Thubten Yeshe and Thubten Zopa Rimpoche. During the course, a Granada TV team visited the Institute for an afternoon, filming and interviewing many people. The five-minute documentary was shown several days later on Granada's 6.00 p.m. news bulletin.

Both Lamas are respected teachers of the Graded Path to Enlightenment and Lam.rim meditation. Lama Thubten Yeshe has been appointed the Institute's Spiritual Director. He was born in Lhasa in 1935. He entered the great monastic college of Sera at the age of six, where he remained up until 1959 and the Communist invasion of Tibet. Whilst at Sera, he underwent all the relevant study and training in Buddhist philosophy and psychology, logic and debate. His scholastic life was coupled with meditation, an important facet of his training and is certified in teaching and assessing the higher meditational states. After his escape from Tibet, he arrived in India, to take up further study and latterly, became the Spiritual Head of the Nepal Mahayana Gompa at Kopan, Nepal, in 1969.

Lama Thubten Zopa Rimpoche was born in Nepal in 1946, near Mount Everest. At the age of seven, he was sent to the monastery of Dromo in east Tibet where he studied Buddhist doctrine and meditation. He resided at Dromo until 1959. After his flight from Tibet, Lama Zopa continued his work at a Tibetan Lama Refugee Camp in north-east India, where he met, and subsequently became closely associated with, Lama Thubten Yeshe. Between them, they directed the activities at the Nepal Mahayana Gompa at Kopan.

When the first course had been completed, a special ceremony was conducted by the Lama's in which the Shrine Room was 'officially' blessed. The Institute, by this time, had conceived of a nucleus in which the principles governing its existence were laid down. This nucleus was defined in two parts – ideologically and practically:

1   *Ideologically by:*
(a) making available to all, the Graduated Path experience of Atisa and Lama Tsongkapa, from beginning to end – Enlightenment.
(b) giving living expression to the Bodhicitta motivation by actualizing a Dharma way of life.

(c) perpetuating the lineage of experience of the Graduated Path in the minds of Western students.

2 *Practically by:*

(a) providing ideal peaceful conditions conducive to the teachings, study and practice of the perfect, pure Mahayana teachings of Guru Shakyamuni.

(b) giving continuous teaching, study, retreat and practical experience opportunity between courses.

(c) making Meditation Courses available to both residents and non-residents at the centre.

(d) existing as a Dharma community serving the needs of the community in the surrounding region by whatever means and in whatever ways possible – spiritually, materially and educationally.

With the first course completed, about a dozen people remained over the winter period with individual visitors coming and going. Now was the time for serious renovation work to begin. Inside, the buildings unsafe structures were demolished in an attempt to stamp out the dry-rot. Outside, an attempt was made to till the fields, weed the pathways and to get down to planting the seeds, which, hopefully, would provide an abundance of vegetables during the coming summer and autumn. A management committee was formed whose function it was to organize the financial and publications side of the Institute.

June of 1976 saw the Institute's first publication from their new home in the guise of a newsletter setting out the growth of the Institute, its facilities, the teachings being offered and its present financial state. For the Institute to be able to push out a newsletter in such a short period of time, with details of its first successful course, in a space of three months, was indeed remarkable. But to me, it signified the energy generated and a solid understanding of the difficult and precarious future ahead – there were no fantasies! Nevertheless, now wasn't the time to be considering an uncertain future in abstract hypothesis.

Within six months of their first full-length course, the Institute managed another during the Christmas vacation which lasted to the first week in January. The course was conducted by a disciple of Geshe Rabten called Gelong Thubten Donyo, an Italian, who taught at the sister centre in Italy. The course, which was dedicated to the Four Noble Truths, was attended by thirty people and was well publicized. This was accentuated by an article which appeared in the *Daily Mail*, the result of a visit by a reporter to the Institute which, again, helped to make public to a wider community the existence of Manjushri. These two events helped thoroughly to establish the Institute as a genuine and durable Buddhist organization to add to the many already confirmed centres throughout Britain.

By February of 1977, the Institute was in a position to look into the future and a synopsis of courses was drawn up running well into the autumn. Also published was a catalogue of books and spiritual paraphernalia, ranging from Thanka posters and incense to glass bead rosaries and Buddharupas; the books were derived from the Tibetan Works and Archives Library in Dharamasala.

Between April and August, the Institute ran many courses and weekend seminars dealing in the main with basic Lam.rim and Buddhist meditation and conducted by such eminent teachers as Ven. Lama Thubten Yeshe, Ven. Lama Thubten Zopa Rimpoche, Ven. Geshe Damcho Yonten and Ven. Gelong Jhampa Kelsang. In August the Institute welcomed Dr Dora Kalff, a Jungian psychologist, who introduced her established 'sand play' method of therapy and analysis. This brought widespread interest as she presented case histories who benefited greatly by adopting this successful analytical technique.

Personal reflections

I think the first thing to strike one on one's arrival is the sheer immensity of not only the property, but the Institute as a whole. To see people living, working and promoting the Dharma is both inspiriting and moving. For as much as the internal structural renovation work is going on all around one, this becomes as good a time as any to reflect on the rapid changes which Buddhism is bringing to our country. In a world where disregard for our fellow men is rife, it is invigorating to retire to a centre like Manjushri and to feel the warmth and harmony that exists in people who are seriously getting down to working on themselves.

Like many other Dharma centres, mindfulness of self and others becomes the motivating force in one's schedule. One tries to live according to the Five Precepts as a basis for further meditative and devotional exercises. I found the daily schedule well balanced and the admixture of meditation, discourses and work (I was more involved in research than any direct participation in the Institute renovation programme), most enjoyable.

Coffee or tea is served at 5.30 a.m. for those anxious enough to present themselves for the Manjushri Puja at 6.00, and, from what I witnessed, most people attended. The puja ran on similar lines to that of most Tibetan pujas – sutra chanting, bell ringing and periods of silence. I thoroughly enjoyed puja even although I didn't stay long enough to grasp completely the significance behind it. At any rate, I always feel, and many people agree with me, that it is the harmonious rhapsody which one experiences at puja which gives it its special reverential flavour. At 8.00 a.m., there is an hour's break for breakfast (vegetarian) followed by Karma Yoga (work in the community) up until noon. Lunch, again totally vegetarian – and very palatable, lasts until 1.00 p.m., after which it is back to the serious and sometimes back-breaking toil of work.

One can acquire a cup of well-earned tea or coffee at 5.00 p.m. in the dining room and a chance to rest one's tired bones until the following day. Lam.rim meditation takes place after tea and lasts for one hour. This is usually conducted by the Institute's Spiritual Director or one of the resident Sangha members. Like the morning puja, I found it a most beautiful session to take part in. The feeling of enchantment is enhanced by the involved commitment shown by the residents and the awe-inspiring atmosphere of the Shrine Room, is second only to that of Samye-Ling's. Supper is at 7.00 and consists of soup, bread and, if the cook is feeling generous, a salad with cheese. This is followed by discussion, which is usually made public by the Secretary.

From what I personally witnessed, I can only see the Institute advance from strength to strength as it is the only Dharma centre in Britain which can present a tripartition of activity, which, I believe, is absolutely essential for the development of the 'complete man'.

Firstly, it combines amongst other things, the involvement of the resident in utilizing this practical skills for the improvement of the centre and hence, the sacrifice of his or her energy in the aid of something else. We in the West, it seems, have become so used to getting something out of our work in life that to be asked to do something for nothing becomes absolutely out of the question. So the unselfish attitude in offering our service for free, helps in negating the ego and overcoming thoughts about gain and loss – ultimately, no one gains – no 'one' loses. Here is karma yoga in action.

Secondly, with the founding of the College, it now means that for those intent on studying Tibetan Buddhism with the objective of deepening their knowledge of the Vajrayana, the Institute can provide the facilities for futhering that ideal. As I mentioned elsewhere, the courses now being offered at the Institute are probably some of the most valuable teaching being offered anywhere in Europe.

Lastly, the Manjushri Institute, with its Western Sangha residents, not to forget its Tibetan ones too, provides one of the most beautiful and peaceful sanctuaries in which to study the Dharma, that to fully appreciate it one must witness it for oneself. To say any more about its beauty, might detract from a phenomenon that surpasses words. My simple advice is this – just go to Manjushri and find out for yourself – you won't be disappointed.

The Lam.rim lineage and doctrines

The Buddha delivered three sets of Dharma teachings after his Enlightenment under the Bodhi Tree at Bodh Gaya. The first began with the *Dharmacakrasutra* at the Deer Park in Sarnarth. The second began with the *Prajnaparamitasutra* at Vultures Peak outside Rajgir. The third began with the preaching of the *Samadhinirmocanasutra* at Vaisali.

The *Prajnaparamitas* are called the 'Mother of the Buddhas', because it is from this fundamental scripture that the two great Mahayana lineages, both of which must be followed in order to gain full Enlightenment, or Buddahood. These two lineages propagate insight into *Sunyata*, and operate widespread action of Bodhicitta and an enlightened attitude of working to be able to liberate all sentient beings from suffering and to ensure their happiness. The enlightened attitude of Bodhicitta is the motivation for the enlightened conduct of a Bodhisattva, an enlightened-bound being to perfect the Paramitas, or Perfections. The *Prajnaparamitas* are preserved in three major recensions. The long version, the *Satasahasrika*, is in 100,000 verses. The middle version, the *Pancavimsatisahasrika*, is in 20,000 verses in Tibetan and 25,000 verses in Sanskrit. The short version, the *Atasahasrika*, is in 8000 verses. These three are called the 'Mother of the Buddhas' – lengthy, medium and short.

After the time of the *Prajnaparamitasutras*, from approximately the second century AD onwards, these two Mahayana lineages split and became separated. The Buddha had transmitted the profound teaching of the insight into SUNYATA to Manjushri, who in turn passed it on to Nagarjuna, the founder of the Madhyamika school. The Buddha had transmitted the teachings of the widespread action of Bodhicitta to Maitreya (the Buddha to come), who in turn passed them on to Asanga, the founder of the Yogacara school. The outstanding Indian teachers who were in the line of those received and transmitted oral tradition teachings, of those two Mahayana lineages include Aryadeva, Candrakirti, Dignaga, Dharmakirti,

Haribadhra and Santideva. The teachings of these lineages flourished, became enriched with experience, and were transmitted at the great Buddhist Monastic Universities of North India, particularly at Nalanda, Vikramasila and Odantapuri.

The two Mahayana lineages were finally recombined in the tenth century AD in the figure of Dipamkara Srijnana Atisa. Having been a disciple to many famous teachers including Santipa and Naropa, Atisa received the teachings of the SUNYATA lineage from Vidyakokila the Elder and Avadhutipa the Younger, and those of the Bodhicitta lineage from Suvarnadvipa and Dharmapala, during his twelve-year sojourn to Sumatra. Having realized how these two lineages held together to form a single harmonious body of teachings without any contradistinctions, Atisa left his position as Abbot of Vikramasila University and travelled to Tibet. Appalled at the widespread belief current at the time that the study of the sutra and the tantra portions of the Buddha's teachings are not necessarily interdependent, Atisa remained in Tibet and composed the *Bodhipathapradipa*, which became the prototype for all subsequent Lam.rim texts. From Atisa and his chief disciple Geshe Dromtonpa, is traced the Kadampa school of Tibetan Buddhism.

Atisa did not transmit all his teachings in their entirety to any one disciple, and consequently there were three subschools of Kadampa which developed. The first emphasized study from oral tradition explanations of the scriptural texts in conjunction with study from the scriptural texts themselves. The second concerned themselves with the study of the oral tradition explanations alone, with reference to the scriptural texts upon which they were originally based. The third school emphasized study along the Graded Path as first written down in the *Bodhipathapradipa*. The outstanding teachers from these Kadampa lines include the four chief disciples of Geshe Dromtonpa and disciples of those.

These fragmented lineages were finally combined in the figure of Lama Je Rimpoche Tsongkapa (1357–1419), the founder of the Gelungpa School of Tibetan Buddhism. Of his forty-five teachers, Je Tsongkapa received the oral tradition teachings. He organized these Lam.rim teachings of the Mahayana lineages, arranged them into a logical sequential order of progressive insights designed to train the mind, annotated them with extensive quotations from standard texts of scriptural authority, and compiled them into three works of varying scholarly scope; the *Lam.rim Chen.mo*; the *Lam.rim ring. ba*; and the *Lam.rim chung.pa*.

The Gelugpa tradition which has followed from Je Tsongkapa still continues to use the Lam.rim teachings as the basis of its monastic education system. The eight Lam.rim texts used are the three Lam.rim texts by Je Tsongkapa plus the Lam.rim by HH the III Dalai Lama (1543–88), the Lam.rim by HH the V Dalai Lama (1617–82), the Lam.rim by the first Panchen Lama (1569–1622), the Lam.rim by the second Panchen Lama (1663–1737) and the Lam.rim of Ngawang D'ag po. The Lam.rim of the Phabongka Rimpoche was compiled following the Lam.rim by the second Panchen Lama. In this composing text, the second Panchen Lama was fulfilling the request made by Je Tsongkapa, who said that he hoped that someone in the future would compile a Lam.rim text designed specifically for meditational practices in accordance with their own meditational experiences. The lineages from the first Phabongka Rimpoche were transmitted to HH the fourteenth Dalai Lama and his tutors. Thus the oral tradition lineage of the Buddha's teachings of SUNYATA and Bodhicitta in the *Prajnaparamitasutras*, has been transmitted through an unbroken succession of Mahayana teachers from Nagarjuna and Asanga, through Atisa and Je Tsongkapa to Geshe Ngawang Dargye and are now existent today in the many Gelugpa centres throughout the world.

The Four Great Meditations

This precious human body

To advance in Vajrayanic practice we must first of all comprehend the rarity of the acquiring of a human body. This body, if we understand how to *use* it – i.e. as a vehicle for transporting us through the sometimes harrowing experience of human existence. The fact that we can only accomplish full, unexcelled Enlightenment in a human body should be enough stimulation for us to direct our energies in this particular direction. But what do we usually end up doing instead? We while away the hours in an endless chain of distractions and trivia, in fact anything but getting down to the immediate work of liberation.

The sum total of lifetimes spent in self-enlightenment is probably incalculable, the same goes for the eons of time in the lower realms. But to have been born in a period in which the sublime teachings of the Buddha have been disseminated is indeed as valuable as a wish-fulfilling gem – we should not throw away this ideal opportunity for advancement in the Dharma. Life is a 'will-o'-the-wisp' appearance, a mirage, a constantly changing flux which, having the power of an electromagnet, entices one to sample her ever changing pantomime.

The precious human body is the product of fructiferous karma which may have taken many lifetimes through suffering, pain and disillusionment. To be totally enlightened requires of us to have been equally disillusioned, and it is this transition of personality which each and every one of us must go through in order to finally and effectively negate the ego and win through to Moksha, or Liberation. So we must daily meditate on this body, feel the boundlessness that it conceals, and what I feel is of the utmost importance, to perceive the immense opportunity for the complete overcoming of suffering it provides – just be in your body – NOW!

Impermanence

The second of these meditations is that of Impermanence. This is a crucial doctrine in Buddhist meditation as so many subsequent teachings are based on this elemental premise. In fact these first two meditations are so complementary to each other, it is sometimes better to observe them together.

In general, we are motivated by the assumption that the so-called lasting possessions of 'ours' is something to be proud of, as something attained by 'us'. But what happens when those attainments of 'ours' are lost, or dissipated, or die? We feel a great loss, suffering ensues and an unsatisfactory feeling engulfs us. To be able to avoid this state of affairs is to develop an acute awareness of the fleeting nature of phenomena in general – to meditate on the actual character of oneself and one's environment becomes the most important facet of one's spiritual life.

To cultivate the faculty of perceiving all conditional phenomena, the perpetual ebb and flow of life's commotion, is to see things in their true perspective and to develop the liberating tool of insight.

One of man's most exacting problems is his building of seemingly well-proportioned social structures on swamp-like foundations. To see impermanency in the permanent is the only 'water-tight' solution to the problem. But in order to bring oneself round to accept this way of seeing means putting one's own 'security' at 'risk'. However, with a sharpened awareness, one soon realises that in fact nothing is, has or ever will be at 'risk', and that the 'letting go' of all preconceived ideas is in the words of Allan Watts finding the 'wisdom of insecurity'. Anicca, as one of the Three Signs of Being, holds a place of highest importance in Buddhist doctrines of all schools, and for that very reason should be meditated on daily in order to awaken in us that special liberating awareness which leads to Enlightenment.

Karma

Karma, although being in the main a practical system in Buddhism, can also be a beneficial subject of meditation. To meditate on Karma is to penetrate the subtle nature and the intricate matrix of causes and effects which manifest daily in our lives. Morality plays a large part in this meditation because the nature of our actions, whether they be good or bad, positive or negative, tend to mould our volitions.

To advance on the Buddhist path, and in the case of Tibetan Buddhism, the Vajrayanic Way, requires of us to adopt a moral and 'centred' way of life to progress in the Dharma. When living within the domain of Karmic law we mystically attune ourselves with the Universal law of the cosmos, where our puerile ego becomes lost in the 'suchness' of existence. A Karmically aware being is a vehicle of the highest compassion and wisdom humanly possible, the personification of Manjushri and Avalokitesvara in human form.

When meditating on Karma, we must strive to promote only good, to scorn the foolish acts which tend to ever more rebirth and to appraise those actions which lead to harmony, good-will and kindness.

Suffering

Suffering forms the last part of the Four Great Meditations. Being the principle tenet in Buddhist philosophy, it constitutes the central core of teaching of all schools, in which the associated elements revolve. To have a profound understanding of this principle, is to perceive reality just as it is, shorn of all its human-contrived conventions. We must constantly meditate on Dukkha to penetrate its deepest mystery, to have compassion for others' sufferings and, if possible, to enlighten others on the liberating effect of the Buddhadharma.

To suffer the effects of past karma, is to realize the latent ignorance which has become our greatest enemy. But if we pause for a moment, it becomes obvious that the ignorance is man-made so to speak, and that in general we are our own worst enemy. The suffering we experience, is more often than not, our dissatisfaction with things previously thought of as pleasant. Our pleasures, likes and dislikes, persuasions and biasedness are constantly changing and for that very reason is a source of suffering. In fact this reasoning can be expanded to include the whole of conditioned phenomena.

It can be assumed from the foregoing that, to understand this basic principle fully requires of us more than an intellectual understanding, but an experiential awareness of what this means in our day to day life. To understand the potential suffering that exists in our attachments to our personal prejudices, and the karmic law which accompanies them. Suffering will always be with us till we learn to awaken to the truth as experienced by our Lord Buddha.

The College of Tibetan Buddhist Studies

In the autumn of 1977, the Institute's College of Tibetan Buddhist Studies was launched, and as far as I know, the first ever of its kind in Britain. Although there have been many spasms of Tibetan teaching in Britain over the past ten years, it still remained necessary for a sequential programme of study for those requiring a day-to-day progressive series of lectures, etc. The Manjushri Institute now hopes to fulfil this need by their new innovatory project.

It is hoped that the courses offered will satisfy what most people would feel to be an intensive academic programme run on similar lines to a university degree course. By breaking up the year into three terms, autumn, spring and summer, the Institute feels that the vacations in between will give the chance for the student to either return to his or her home, or to continue to stay on at the Institute and partake in the inter-term courses which deal in the main with Lim.ram practice and associated subjects.

I don't think it in the least discreditable to assume that in the future there is the distinct possibility that a degree course could be offered at the Institute – and if not a degree, then at least a diploma. This would give the would-be aspirant the chance to continue on an equal footing with their university counter-parts and to go on and try for their PhD. Sometimes I feel that we in Britain are a little complacent when it comes to offering academic courses in Buddhism in our universities. I'm sure that if it can be accomplished in America and Canada, and I must add, with the greatest success, then there should be no reasons why it couldn't be introduced here in Britain. After all, Buddhism has had a much longer and distinguished history in Britain than in our transatlantic neighbours.

The academic year will be broken up into two areas of study; courses in Buddhism (Tibetan) based on the College's syllabus and the inter-term courses in specific Lam.rim subjects and associated themes.

It should be understood that the following subjects are purely tentative and that an established synopsis will take some time in compiling based on several years of experience.

Autumn Term: Entering the Path to Enlightenment
(Bodhicaryavatara), by Shantideva

The autumn term begins with the study of this absorbing text by the enlightened Indian monk who taught at the famous Buddhist University of Nalanda. This brilliant text encloses the *summum bonum* of all Mahayana philosophy and is reputed to have been written in the eighth century. The text is unique in that philosophical intellection is dismissed and is replaced by the down to earth problems of our own illusion and suffering. This is ideally represented and exemplified by Shantideva's own enlightened lifestyle.

This course is open, like most of the other courses, to both beginners and more advanced students, but I feel that it would be more suited to those who are committed to the Mahayana ideal. The course will be structured to comprise of two lectures per day, six days a week, and it would be most advisable to attend every lecture.* Unlike basic university courses, where much of the material could be gleaned from books, the contents of this course is exclusive and not so easily

---

*The course tutor who will lecture at each term course will be the Venerable Geshe Kelsang Gyatso, the Spiritual Programme Director of the Institute, and a highly realized meditation master from Tibet.

acquired in bookshops, etc. This course will last for ten weeks.

Spring Term: The mental factors

In January of each year, the spring term will commence. The 1978 syllabus programmed the above subject as the second part of the yearly academic study. From the title, the mental factors, it can be inferred that the subject deals with Buddhist psychology. In this course each factor will be outlined in detail, and slotted into its own particular category in the mental constitution of man's mind. To have a deep understanding of Buddhist psychology is to learn to know how our own mind works – and if we know this, we are half way there in the ultimate control of our speech and actions. Throughout this course, each student is required to attend all the lectures, as to miss out in any could prove impracticable in the understanding of further subjects.

A Treatise on the Middle Path (Madhyamikavatara, chapters 1 to 5), by Chandrakirti

The second half of the spring term continues with the study of Chandrakirti's *Madhyamikavatara*. This engrossing text is a commentary on the profound philosophy of Nagarjuna (second century AD), who, apart from Shankara and Buddha Shakyamuni himself, must rank as one of the greatest minds to have walked on Indian soil. Briefly, the course deals with the concept, and I use that expression very loosely, of Sunyavada, or the 'Doctrine of the Void'. Here, all philosophical propositions about the eternalistic or nihilistic nature of reality are totally swept aside. Instead, the meditator aims at avoiding all extremities of categorical expression and resides in the bliss of silent, non-dual Liberation.

As with the course on the Mental Factors, each student is required to attend all the lectures. The spring term constitutes eight weeks of study.

Summer Term: The Graduated Path to Enlightenment,
(Lam.rim Chen.mo), by Lama Tsongkapa

The summer term is broken up into two parts, each of four weeks' duration. Lama Tsongkapa's *Lam.rim Chen.mo* is a celebrated text in Tibetan Buddhism, and again, it's not the kind of text easily available in the West. The College offers this important course as a basis for those wishing to study the complete path leading to Enlightenment. This beautiful text presents a way of life which is designed for those without great incisive mental abilities, and is especially simple to follow as each stage of the path is equated to the individual's spiritual state. Lama Je Tsongkapa, is only one in a successive lineage of fully realized teachers, and it is because of this that the text under study is so important to us in the West.

It should be noted that the student may attend whichever half of the course he wishes – but whichever half he attends, it is important that he or she attends all of the lectures.

Inter-Term Courses and Services

Throughout the academic year, the College will be running an assortment of courses, many of which will be of interest to those without any Buddhist persuasions. Again, these courses are purely tentative and are not to be taken as being in any way final. I am listing them here so that the reader can have an appreciation of the facilities offered and the first-class services available at the Institute.

Christmas vacation: The Graduated Path to Enlightenment

This will be a condensed form of the summer term course and will act as a reminder for those who found the subject too difficult the first time round. The course will be run by a German monk resident at the Institute, Gelong Kunchog Sherab.

Easter vacation

The Easter vacation course will be run by the Ven. Geshe Rabten, the representative of HH the Dalai Lama in Europe. This course may also be run by Gelong Jampa Kelsang.

Summer vacation

The provisional syllabus for the summer vacation course is as follows:

I   The Graduated Path to Enlightenment. (Lam.rim) 2 weeks
II   Initiation and Instruction in Yoga Tantra★ 2 weeks
III   Instruction in Guru Yoga★ 12 days
IV   Guided Group Retreats 2 weeks

Each course will be run by one of the Institute's leading Sangha members and also Ven. Thubten Yeshe and Ven. Thubten Zopa Rimpoche.

Western psychology and psychotherapy

Here is an already-established course at the Institute dealing with Jungian psychotherapy in its relation to Buddhism. This course is conducted by Dr Dora Klaff, a member of the International Society of Jungian Analysts, and a personal friend of the late Dr Carl Gustav Jung. This course will be offered during the summer vacation where students will be introduced to Frau Klaff's 'sand play' technique in mental therapy.

This is a ten-day course and will be of particular interest to psychologists, psychiatrists and social workers.

Apart from the main term-time and inter-term courses, the Institute will be offering many week-end seminars ranging from Buddhist meditation to Christianity and Western Mysticism.

The Institute has on offer three main social services which

★These courses are open only to those who have previously attended a Lam.rim course and are engaged in Dharma practice.

are designed to aid the Dharma student in his comprehension of the teachings. Firstly, there is the Tibetan Art class, where the student will be introduced to basic Thanka painting. The objective is not to produce skilled Tibetan artists, the minimum period of time in learning this artform is about seven years anyway, but to give the student an appreciation of this highly evolved system of art.

Secondly, one can also study the Tibetan language which is of particular use to those reciting Tibetan texts in their daily pujas. The course would also be of value to those who aspire to translatory work and, incidentally, to philologists who have a leaning to Oriental languages.

Lastly, the Institute can provide facilities for those wishing to make retreat. The only provision is that the would-be meditator make prior arrangements with the Institute, providing a schedule advised by a qualified teacher.

If there has been one course which has intrigued me it must be the one on drug dependency called simply, 'Kick the Habit'. This course will be run by a qualified doctor and quite naturally will concentrate on those people who have a drug problem, whether it be in its early stages or has deteriorated to chronic proportions. Basically, the course will concentrate on the nature of the mind and the ways in which one becomes dependent on drugs in order to continue a 'normal' life. The remedies to this problem will be discussed and several techniques issued for the use of those in this state of illness.

For information about this and preceding courses, contact the Institute, pages 211–12.

A Sense of Universal Responsibility:
The XIVth Dalai Lama's Message to the West

In 1973, an historic occasion took place in the West which, I presume, many people were unaware of. This was of course the visit of HH the Dalai Lama to the West – the first time in history. The effect of his visit may never be known, such is spiritual lustration. But if the West is suffering from spiritual amnesia, then His Holiness's expostulations are surely an ambrosial remedy fit for the Gods.

During his visits to eleven West European countries, the same theme kept recurring time and again, namely, the responsibility of each and every one of us to cultivate what His Holiness calls 'a sense of universal responsibility and a good heart'.

At the end of his European tour, His Holiness came to London in October 1973 and was received at the Buddhist Society by Mr Christmas Humphreys and Lt-Col. Gunter-Jones. At a reception held in his honour, His Holiness delivered an inspired lecture on the spiritual, religious and world problems facing the world and the need to adopt a spiritual approach to alleviate them. Whilst in London, he also visited the Tibet Society, the Buddhapadipa Temple and the London Buddhist Vihara. As can be expected with the emergence of such a dignitary in this country, the whole proceedings were extensively covered by the press, journals and television.

However, I am not going to dwell on His Holiness's itinerary as this would be just so many descriptions of functions and receptions which, when you come to think of it, were all of the same format and homogeneity. Instead, I would rather outline this message of the Dalai Lama as I feel it is of lasting consequence to us in the West who, at present, are in dire need of a way, a path of spiritual development to counterbalance our technological expertise.

His Holiness has stressed that there is no elemental difference between East and West for all the cultural, geographical and historical dissimilarities. This, according to His Holiness, is a fabrication, an unfortunate result of a priority of values which, on the face of it, has divided humanity. His Holiness explains:

Such differences as seem to exist are superficial and superimposed in many ways which cannot and should not separate man from man. Whenever I meet 'foreigners', I feel there is no barrier between us; to me such meetings are man to man relationships, heart-to-heart contacts.*

*Universal Responsibility and the Good Heart, by HH the Dalai Lama, Library of Tibetan Works and Archives, 1974.

The individual problems of man are mirrored in a broader plane in a nation's constitution. The effects of these problems are felt at personal and communal levels, and according to the quality of the individual, the community will either be benefited or harmed. But, sometimes a nation's problems become an international affair, such as we see today, and because of this it is critically important that goodwill prevails and compassion dominates:

One nation's problems can no longer be solved by itself entirely or satisfactorily, because much depends on the attitude and co-operation of other nations.*

The doctrine of compassion in Mahayana Buddhism is tantamount to complete Enlightenment. This is no undescried territory, but the latent and deepest of human qualities which a human being possesses. It resides at the centre of our being and is a quality to be refined. This compassion, or the genuine concern for others can only blossom when we negate our own welfare and security. Most people speak and act from the egocentric mirage of 'I', the perpetual desire for self-aggrandizement and selfishness. The Dalai Lama speaks from an Enlightened centre devoid of clinging and attachments:

If we are able to develop a better understanding among ourselves, then on the basis of that understanding we can share and try to overcome the suffering of others and achieve happiness for others. Happiness for yourself comes automatically as a result of this concern for others. I feel the few should be willing to sacrifice for the many. Let us compare ourselves, you and I: you are clearly in the majority while I am a single individual. Therefore I consider you [audience] are much more important than myself, because you are in the majority.†

The Dalai Lama is the human personification of Chenresigs, the Bodhisattva of Compassion and it is this identity which gives His Holiness such authority and dynamism. The compassion which His Holiness refers to is not alas, the love we

Universal Responsibility and the Good Heart, p. 5.
†*Ibid.*, p. 6.

may have for a close one or the lustfulness for one of the opposite sex but the undifferentiated compassion without discrimination for our enemies. It could be compared to the 'turn the
other cheek' philosophy of Christianity but very few cultivate
this quality such is our attachment to the ego. We live in a
period of dour materialism but, paradoxically enough, an era
of great spiritualism. The West is wakening to a reality never
conceived of in its past history and this reality is skilfully
displayed in the Mahayana (Great Vehicle) school of Buddhism.
In the Mahayana we not only aspire to Enlightenment for
ourselves but for all living beings. His Holiness has decreed:

According to the Mahayana School of Buddhism you must not
only think in terms of human beings in this regard but of all sentient
beings. And ultimately all sentient beings have the potentiality of
attaining Buddhahood.*

And referring to the qualities which should be cultivated in
the realization of this state, His Holiness continues:

If you have (the inner qualities of) compassion love and respect
for others, honesty and humility – then you can call yourself a real
human being. Anger, attachment, hatred, jealousy and pride, all
these bad qualities are our common enemies.†

Tibet was a country which encouraged spiritual advancement to technological sophistication and up to recent times
was, to a certain extent, backward in its scientific development.
But on the other hand, the phenomenal religious culture which
has been the bastion in Tibetan religious history for thirteen
centuries is immeasurable. The mental and spiritual evolution
of an isolated race like Tibet has in the past fifteen years
become the centre of attraction for millions of Truth seekers
in the West. I suppose the happy medium would be a balanced
and harmonious existence as the two must complement each
other before true equilibrium can become manifest. The
Dalai Lama does not scorn scientific development like some
religious leaders do. He advised:

*Ibid.
†Ibid., p. 9.

I see nothing wrong with material progress that provided man takes precedence over progress. In fact it has been my firm belief that in order to solve human problems in all their dimensions we must be able to combine and harmonise external material progress with inner mental development.*

In the following pages I have taken several questions from *Universal Responsibility and the Good Heart* which were put to His Holiness on his visit – the answers I think are of perennial importance and should be adhered to with humility.

Universal responsibility

'*His Holiness spoke continually on cultivating a universal attitude towards our fellow men, but by what means and in which way does one go about cultivating this attitude – and what part does Buddhism play in achieving this?*'

'I am fully convinced that there is a great need for this development of universal responsibility. I also feel that there is many ways and methods of trying to develop this kind of feeling and as yet I am still trying to find which method would be most suitable.'

and

'Another way, which I basically think is the most important, is this feeling for others, a feeling of closeness, trying to share the sufferings of others. In my opinion these are the two ways of achieving this universal responsibility. But the most important responsibility lies on the younger generation; an educational system where there is bad influence should be avoided as far as possible. For example when you see too much violence on television or other mediums of the mass media, I feel that it has great influence on the person.'†

'*This universal responsibility must be based on some kind of values, a morality, a premise comprising good-will and respect. But what does His Holiness feel about this matter?*'

*Ibid.
†pp. 16 and 17.

'I feel the basis is that every one of us do not want suffering and every one of us want something comfortable or happy in life. There is a verse which says that just as your physical body would not like the slightest pain, so you have to realise that the other being also has a similar feeling. For example, when you talk about rights, like the human rights, the question is what do these rights fundamentally boil down to. Fundamentally it boils down to the feeling of "I" and on the basis of that feeling you want happiness and bliss and you do not want suffering. And just as you have these desires, your fellow being has similar desires; therefore what you have the right to, it is not correct to say that others do not have the right to. On the basis of these rights, that you have and the rights that others have, if you believe these are similar, then others have rights also. Now if you compare which is the most important, you are just one single person whereas the other is limitless. There are thousands of millions of people, therefore the others are much more important, because you are just one individual. I feel this way of thinking is a democratic way of religion.'*

Happiness

Every mortal being desires happiness; it is a natural instinct which motivates people and itself is a characteristic of life sought by each and every one of us. But true happiness, in other words, lasting happiness is something not so easily attained. This is not the contentedness of family life, the passing pleasures of the senses or the fame and fortune which goes with big business life. What I refer to is the ineffable bliss which comes with the fruition of a morally, taint-free and contemplative life. The happiness of one who has led such a life cannot be discerned by materalistic values. However, many of us, in fact most of us have to be content with lesser attainments. His Holiness gives his view on the way and the goal:

'Yes, there are various kinds of happiness. Certain happiness, like bliss, is something much more deep, but the deeper or higher happiness or inner bliss cannot be achieved by the masses. A few individuals can achieve this, mainly through the Christian belief

*pp. 17 and 18.

in God – as a Buddhist there are certain methods to achieve this higher bliss or happiness. But I am talking of general happiness, the real peace of the world and the combination of mental peace and worldly progress. If we have this feeling (of universal responsibility), then I am quite sure we can solve many problems that right way through peaceful means. This is my main topic for discussion. I realise that it is rather difficult to make a good human being, but despite that it is worthwhile to try. It may take fifty, eighty or a hundred years, but as I am a religious person I feel it is reasonable to think this way and to try.'*

Tibetan Buddhism in the West

The rise and influx of Tibetan Buddhism in the West in recent years has become, at least to many young people, a welcomed refuge from an artificial and convention-ridden society based on all the wrong labels. When one assesses the world economy for instance, it becomes glaringly obvious that when a WHO conference on food control talks of malnutrition and starvation whilst all the delegates sit down at lunch-time to a multi-course meal – and can only at the hinder end stump up enough money to keep the stomachs of five million starving children in Bangladesh and Ethiopia full for a day, then there is something chronically wrong with our democracies. This is only one example of the kind of society that this very special form of Buddhism has been introduced to. But could Buddhism offer us genuine spiritual help and liberation in this kind of environment? The Dalai Lama seems to think it can:

'For some people it would be of benefit because for religion there is no national boundary. Even among Tibetans we have Christians as well as Moslems. We are all the same. What is important is the faith or religion which is more suitable to you.'

'But will the values of Buddhism be useful in the West?'

'Religion is something for all men, it is a common property, there are no man-made boundaries for that. It should be used for any people or for any person for whom it may be found beneficial.

*pp. 28 and 29.

I believe that each religion has its own qualities, its own values. Also for these past many centuries the various different kinds of religion have benefited, in their own way, the many different kinds of people on this earth.'*

The Future

The future is of immediate importance to us, if not on an ultimate level then on a relative level. The majority of human beings tend to worry, philosophize and plan for an uncertain future which daily becomes more impersonal the more we advance in technological and scientific development. Whereas the materialist, because of his logical and mechanical training, would forecast a comfortable future ahead based on scientific discoveries which has brought the possibility of a nuclear holocaust to our doorstep, the spiritually developed man would pronounce a future of progress towards universal responsibility in spiritual and inter-racial co-operation. But what does His Holiness think about the future:

'It seems to me that this present atmosphere of the world is not very happy. Generally you know what is right and what is wrong, yet despite this knowledge, you almost always take the opposite action; because of the pressure, of the atmosphere, you cannot act in the right way. So from my view-point at least this is not very beneficial, but we can change this. Therefore I have more hope in the future, the younger generation. As I mentioned before, the goal or the aim is happiness for everyone. All mankind desires a happy life. In order to achieve that goal different people adopt different methods. Some people try to achieve it through science and technology, some through religious practices and some through different government systems, different ideologies. If we look at the main goal, then all the others are different methods to reach that goal.'†

A Message for Today

But what of today? The Dalai Lama, after his successful trip

*pp. 18 and 19.
†p. 28.

to the West, found in this half of the globe much to enthuse over. People, especially the young, were beginning to ask themselves which way does one follow, who to believe in a world where everybody has supposedly the correct answers to life's eternal problems. His Holiness, when asked the question about the aspects of life which makes him optimistic about the future, gave a brief and simple explanation which we in the West should take particularly seriously:

'I believe that this solution, the combination of inner development and the material progress, is actually connected with the very survival of man himself. If in society, there is no justice no truth, if everything is done by money and power, then it is rather difficult to live. Sometimes this atmosphere does have great influence. There are many good systems, for example democracy, and in each system there are many good points. Of course there are many bad points also, mostly caused by money and power. As human beings we must live on this earth not for our generation but for the next one, so if there is really no justice and no truth, then it would be very sad and very unfortunate. As Easterners we have many problems like poverty and disease, lack of education. In the West you are highly developed in the material sense, the living standard is very high, which is very important, very good. Yet despite these facilities you have mental unrest, for example amongst the youth and among politicians. This is not a healthy sign; it is a clear indication that there is something wrong, something lacking. So this is my theme and because of it I am a little optimistic.'*

*p. 29.

6 Friends of the Western Buddhist Order — a New Concept in Buddhism

Buddhism is a way of life that leads to a spiritual experience, in fact to a number of experiences. These experiences link up into a series that culminates in the supreme experience of Nirvana.

SANGHARAKSHITA*

The Friends of the Western Buddhist Order is perhaps the most unique Buddhist organization of its kind in the West. Essentially a spiritual community, it has taken the fifth step of the Noble Eightfold Path, namely, Right Livelihood, as the most co-operative way of spreading Dharma. By means of its Order of Upasakas (male) and Upasikas (female), the 'Friends' are disseminating and propagating the Dharma through an interdependent structure of communities and centres. The Order, which has over one hundred fully ordained members, follow the teachings of the Ven. Maha Sthavira Sangharakshita. Before going into the framework of the movement, I think it profitable if we first take a look at the life of the man who made it all possible.

Ven. Sangharakshita, or Bhante, as he is more popularly known, is an Englishman who spent twenty years of his life in India as a Buddhist monk. Born in London in 1925, Bhante was sixteen when he realized that he was a Buddhist, as a result of reading *The Diamond Sutra* (Vajracchedika Prajnaparamita) and *The Sutra of Hui Neng*. Two years later he came across the

*Sayings, Poems, Reflections, FWBO, 1976.

journal of the Buddhist Society, then known as *Buddhism in England*, whereupon he began visiting the Society and met its President Christmas Humphreys. He began attending meetings and before long acquired all the basic fundamental doctrines of this great religion; this was 1942 to 1944.

In 1943, Bhante was conscripted into the army and spent three years on active service in India, Ceylon and Singapore. This enabled him to savour the teachings of Buddhism first hand. In 1946 he left the army, tore up all his documents and for a time wandered through India as a renunciate. Throughout this period he met a number of spiritual teachers and the thought of ordination into the Buddhist Sangha gradually became uppermost in his mind. After concluding his pilgrimage to the most important Buddhist holy sites of India, Bhante took the lower ordination from a Theravadin monk who named him Sangharakshita (Protector of the Order). A year later he took the higher ordination at Sarnath and at this point he could not be said to be following the teachings of any one school of Buddhism exclusively.

By 1957, Bhante felt the need for a permanent headquarters from which to work and promote the Dharma. This need was fulfilled when he established the Triyana Vardhana Vihara or, 'The Monastery of the Three Ways' in Kalipong, where he had lived since 1950. For the next seven years Bhante worked from this Vihara diligently and compassionately aiding in the ex-untouchable movement of conversion to Buddhism which had originally been launched by the late Dr Ambedkar. For twelve years he was editor of the *Maha Bodhi Journal*, the voice of the Maha Bodhi Society of India. He received many Tantric initiations from Nyingmapa lamas as well as some valuable teaching from the Ch'an Buddhist yogi C. M. Chen, and finally received the Bodhisattva Precepts from Dhardo Rimpoche as the culmination of his Mahayana ordination.

Bhante at this time was totally happy with his lot in India – his own Temple, teachers and a stream of Westerners seeking spiritual guidance. For several years prior to his return to the West, Bhante literally delivered hundreds of lectures on the

F

Dharma, performed all sorts of spiritual and ordination ceremonies and worked tirelessly for Buddhism in India. But in August 1964, Bhante accepted an invitation from the Sangha Trust at the Hampstead Buddhist Vihara, London to stay and help out in their attempts to teach Dharma. Bhante agreed to stay for four months. However, due to the interest shown, not only from the people visiting the Vihara, but from the Buddhist Society as well, he extended his stay to two years. But even after two years Bhante was still not satisfied; Buddhism was still not changing people's lives. Their outlook on life was the same – in other words Buddhism in Britain at this time was not dynamic enough. So the need for a deeper Buddhist life was felt by Bhante, something different, a new direction with regenerated principles.

Bhante decided to revisit India in 1967 and to seek out his teachers and ask their advice. His stay lasted for five months, during which time he toured India prior to returning to London. On his arrival back in the West Bhante decided that a new and reformed group was needed which would ideally revolve around a 'monastic' centre. This new movement would basically be non-sectarian as far as doctrine was concerned and would attempt to become financially self-sufficient. The yellow-robed, shaven-headed, umbrella-carrying bhikkhu was the last thing which Bhante envisaged. To be a monastic community in the West meant a completely new structure and an amended code of conduct. There would be none of the window dressing and decorative façade which Bhante saw so much of in the East.

During April of 1967, Bhante began his new movement in a humble basement floor of a Japanese shop called Sakura in Monmouth Street, London. The movement's centre was a small room containing a Triyana Shrine where the meditation classes were held every Thursday. In fact the meditational aspect of the movement was, and still is, the central core running through every FWBO centre. In those early days lectures and seminars took place at Centre House, Kensington and open retreats at Haslemere. Bhante himself began lecturing to ever-growing numbers of people and it became obvious that a larger centre was desperately needed.

After five years at Sakura, which was by now a Buddhist shop, the search for new premises was instigated. The FWBO movement by this time took on a less secular appearance with the first group of Upsaka ordinations. The event took place on Saturday 6 April 1968 at Sakura. These were private ordinations where Bhante imparted the Refuges and Precepts along with a mantra, and a new name to the individual. The following evening at Centre House, the public ordinations were held. Attending the ceremony were two Thai bhikkhus and a Zen priest which added to the traditional flavour of the ordinations.

A few years later, a large building was found at 1a Balmore Street, Archway, London which was to be, at least, the temporary centre for future FWBO developments and was named Pundarika. The Order's activities dramatically increased with the inclusion of Pujas, celebrations, Hatha yoga classes, karate and retreats. There was also the programme of lectures by Bhante which fulfilled the lives of the Order Members.

For the first year and a half, Bhante conducted all the lectures and classes single-handed until fledgeling Order Members were able to cope with and teach Dharma. In 1973, Bhante withdrew from direct involvement with the movement and went into retreat in Cornwall for a year. Here Bhante devoted most of his time to literary pursuits and the completion of the memoirs of his life in India, *The Thousand-Petalled Lotus*.

With Bhante's absence, a consolidation and intensification of energy emerged within the Order. The spirit of Buddhism which emanated from Bhante grew rapidly within the Order Members, a phenomena which was fully tested during Bhante's absence. The inevitable expansion followed as a matter of course and soon the FWBO centres sprang up and established themselves in Norwich, Brighton, Surrey, Glasgow and also in north, west and east London. It also became apparent that a sensible and realistic attitude about existence, in the economic sense of the word, was soberly accepted by the individual centres' leading Order Members. Gone was the romantic image of the Sangha of the East; and here was the development and adaptation of a Westernized, fully self-sufficient unit.

The movement as a whole is founded on youth and is representative of the avidity in which the young people of Britain have taken to Buddhism. In the F W B O the Upasakas and Upasikas, as well as the Mitras* are given complete autonomy in which to direct their talents for the benefit of the Dharma. This has led to such enterprises as artists' studios, printing presses, wholefood stores, vegetarian restaurants, book and journal publications, yoga, crafts, bookshops, building businesses and many more.

As mentioned elsewhere there are now over a hundred Upasakas and Upasikas in the Order and before going further I would like to turn to the role played by these people within the F W B O. Principally these are men and women who have committed themselves to the Three Jewels, the Buddha, Dharma and Sangha. They have come to the conclusion that they want to evolve, and that further spiritual evolution requires that they change. This change can only come about with the opening up of a path, a direction and a goal – a goal which is none other than Enlightenment itself. Not unlike any other Buddhist, the 'Friends' follow the Dharma in which to perpetuate this change. But in order to change, it sometimes helps to befriend those who are into changing the same way, using the same 'instruments'; hence the Sangha.

In the Upasaka ordination, the recipient vows to observe ten Precepts within which his moral and spiritual development will grow. In Buddhism the Precepts are of major significance because spiritual advancement can only take place on the unshakable foundations of morality. There are several permutations of the Precepts which change from school to school, but within the F W B O the following are observed: abstention from killing, or taking life; abstention from stealing,

*A close friend of the Order and one attracted to possible ordination into the movement.

or taking that which is not given; abstention from sexual misconduct; abstention from falsehood, or from saying that which is untrue; abstention from idle talk, or gossip; verbal devaluation of others, or back-biting and harsh or slanderous speech; and lastly, abstention from greed, hatred and wrong, or false views. However, two changes generally take place to Order Members who undertake the observance of the Precepts. Firstly, the pressures of observing the Precepts 'in the world', or trying to hold down a job in the city, become very great. So working full time in the Order's Right Livelihood activities becomes most necessary. And secondly, as the momentum of the spiritual life develops within oneself, a strong desire, or even sacrifice, to give one's life to the Buddha, Dharma and Sangha is poignantly evident. Because of this Order Members are observing strict Right Livelihood and are existing on £7.00 to £8.00 a week.

Their main work consists in running classes and retreats, bringing out publications, delivering lectures, prison visiting and intrinsically committing themselves to Dharma life. There are also some, who, at the time of ordination had responsibilities in the form of families, and, naturally, they have to honour those responsibilities. However, although living at home, etc., they keep in close contact with other Order Members via the weekly Order meeting. It transpires that Bhante sees no spiritual distinction between the monk, in the old-fashioned sense and the layman as such. The important point which should be borne in mind is the commitment to the Three Jewels.* Whether you be a householder or a communal Order Member, both are still one inseparable spiritual community, *living* in different ways but with the same spiritual dedication. The F W B O does not believe in purely informal monasticism as can be witnessed in the East, a spectacle which can be so artificial.

Over the years a network of F W B O centres and communities have grown, a phenomenon which adequately portrays the actual intensity of energy running throughout the whole

*See *The Three Jewels, an Introduction to Buddhism*, Windhorse Publications, 1977.

THE FWBO NETWORK

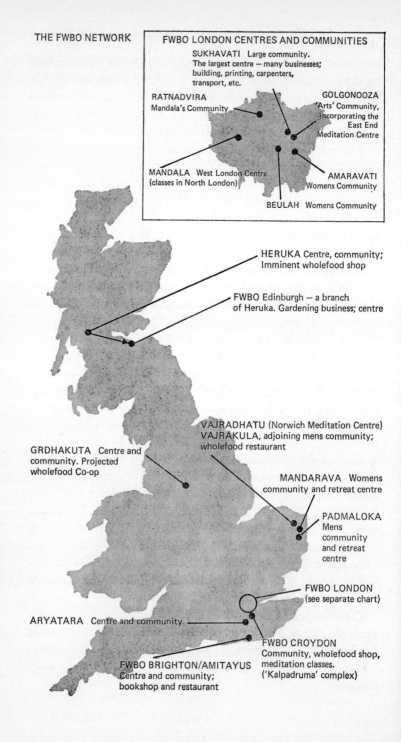

FWBO LONDON CENTRES AND COMMUNITIES

SUKHAVATI Large community.
The largest centre — many businesses;
building, printing, carpenters,
transport, etc.

RATNADVIRA
Mandala's Community

GOLGONOOZA
'Arts' Community,
incorporating the
East End
Meditation Centre

MANDALA West London Centre
(classes in North London)

AMARAVATI
Womens Community

BEULAH Womens Community

HERUKA Centre, community;
Imminent wholefood shop

FWBO Edinburgh — a branch
of Heruka. Gardening business; centre

VAJRADHATU (Norwich Meditation Centre)
VAJRAKULA, adjoining mens community;
wholefood restaurant

GRDHAKUTA Centre and
community. Projected
wholefood Co-op

MANDARAVA Womens
community and retreat centre

PADMALOKA
Mens
community
and retreat
centre

FWBO LONDON
(see separate chart)

ARYATARA Centre and community.

FWBO CROYDON
Community, wholefood shop,
meditation classes.
('Kalpadruma' complex)

FWBO BRIGHTON/AMITAYUS
Centre and community;
bookshop and restaurant

FWBO movement. The following pages outline this growth and gives an insight into this new Buddhist direction which is the Friends of the Western Buddhist Order.

The FWBO Brighton, Amitayus

In January of 1975 the FWBO established a centre in Brighton which was later named Amitayus (The Lord of Boundless Life). Previously, the group operated as a branch of FWBO, North London. However, on 1 August 1976, FWBO Brighton became an autonomous centre within the movement and subsequently became a registered charity in June 1977.

At present there are four Order Members resident in the Community/Centre, two Upasakas and two Upasikas. The Centre's Right Livelihood activities consist of a wholefood vegetarian restaurant called 'Sunrise', and 'The Windhorse Bookshop'. There are proceedings under way to have established a co-op to be named 'Vajra Enterprises' which will include the above-mentioned businesses as well as a projected removals business, a toy-making 'factory' and a joinery/building service.

The Centre presently runs two meditation classes per week, one for beginners and one for the more advanced. These commence at 7.15 p.m. on Mondays and Tuesdays and are free of charge. On Thursday evenings the Centre offers a Meditation and Basic Buddhism Course. The course basically deals with meditation theory and practice and includes full instructions on how to meditate. Running concurrently is the Basic Buddhism class which deals in the main with the fundamentals of Buddhist doctrine. This course costs £6.50 for the eight weeks' duration.

Wednesdays are given over to two Hatha Yoga courses, one for beginners, the other for advanced students. This ten-week course costs £6.50. On Friday evenings the Centre has the weekly Order meeting open only to Upasakas and Upasikas.

Community living is encouraged at Brighton and plans are under way to have another men's community established soon.

The Centre also runs retreats which are usually held at an independent setting on the outskirts of Brighton itself.

The FWBO Glasgow, Heruka

The Glasgow Community/Centre grew out of the earlier Glasgow Buddhist Group, and became in July 1973, the Friends of the Western Buddhist Order, Glasgow. The earlier group was founded in 1968 after the inspiration injected by Chogyam Trungpa. A couple of people who had attended Trungpa's lectures got together fortnightly to meditate and study Dharma. After a period of years a 'hard core' of dedicated Buddhists asserted themselves and invited an FWBO Order Member, Upasika Gotami, to organize the first FWBO centre in Scotland. This came to fruition when in July 1973 the FWBO Glasgow was formed with its headquarters at 246 Bath Street. Later, several Order Members from the south were invited to Scotland to get things moving.

In February 1976, owing to financial difficulties, the group left Bath Street and took up temporary residence in a Glasgow Corporation Council House. Here they functioned until April 1977. The 'new' Centre was located in Nithsdale Road on the south side of the city and, for a time, numbers dropped and interest flagged. By this time the Centre was supporting an Order of four Upasakas and one Upasika.

If nothing else, Glasgow had its own 'real life' FWBO Sangha, a foundation which kept a small light shining in the face of total collapse. Because of the structurally unsound state of the building, the group were invited to vacate the premises. This led to a complete halt to FWBO activities in Glasgow, at least from a communal point of view. Meetings continued on a small scale at various locations in Glasgow but the communal–spiritual centre was missing.

During this crucial period, fund-raising activities were stepped up in anticipation of purchasing a property. Due to generous donations and loans, the FWBO were at last, after two and a half years, able to buy a spacious flat at Kelvinside

Terrace South. In October 1977, the Order Members moved into their new Centre which was aptly named Heruka. Classes which had previously been attended by half a dozen people increased to about sixty for the meditation sessions.

Heruka's Right Livelihood activities are now moving again especially their future wholefood shop.

The FWBO Norwich, Vajradhatu and Vajrakula

The first FWBO activities in Norfolk began in January 1976, when an Order Member, Upasaka Devamitra, in conjunction with three other Order Members began organizing Yoga classes in a school hall in Norwich. By April that year, premises were found in Queens Road, whereupon immediate renovation work began in an attempt to bring the house up to presentable standards. The Centre officially opened on 12 September. One year later, however, a more central and substantial premises were found which subsequently led to the forming of the Norwich Meditation Centre at 41a All Saints Green, Norwich. This title was adopted for publicity reasons and generally goes under the name of Vajradhatu.

In February 1977 a men's community was founded next door at 41b All Saints Green and was officially named Vajrakula. This was the first community in the movement's history to refuse entry of women onto its premises. The community can accommodate between six and eight people. When Vajrakula found its feet, two Order Members moved back to Queens Road and opened a Buddhist arts workshop, concentrating their energy on Tanka painting and casting Buddharupas.

Norwich was provided with its first ever vegetarian restaurant when in January 1977 the FWBO opened the Rainbow Restaurant. Right Livelihood is here sustained by a number of Order Members. But at present larger premises are sought in which a separate coffee bar will be opened day and night. Also within the same premises, Yoga classes and poetry readings are scheduled in order to provide an informal contact with the public.

At present there are four Upasakas and one Upasika committed to the Norwich Meditation Centre. Current activities at the Centre include regular six-week meditation courses accommodating twenty people at a time. These are followed by courses introducing basic Buddhism to the enquirer. Also currently on the programme are meditation/Puja and Dharma study groups for men and women Mitras alongside the weekly Order meeting. There are also the occasional week-end retreat and communication course. Also from time to time some of the Order Members deliver private and public lectures to outside groups.

Padmaloka

Padmaloka is the men's retreat Centre and Community situated in the small village of Surlingham, near Norwich, Here Bhante has settled in permanent residence around a strong community of Order Members. Lesingham House also houses the Office of the Western Buddhist Order where the archives of the FWBO movement are kept.

The community was formed in 1976 and is divided into two sectors, one half for Order Members and the other for retreat residents. Padmaloka is essentially a Community-cum-Retreat Centre and has resident about a dozen Upasakas at any one time. Right Livelihood activities are kept down to a minimum although a candle-making 'factory' has been established for some time. The candles which are manufactured are distributed to all FWBO branches and craft shops up and down the country.

There are basically two different kinds of retreat held at Padmaloka, one dealing with Dharma study, the other with Ordination. Both are run by Order Members and contain regular meditation and Puja sessions. The Dharma study retreats tend to be devoted to the study of two currently popular sutras – the Bodhicaryavatara by Santideva, and the Udana, a very old Pali sutta. As can be expected all, retreats held at the Centre are for men only, which helps to alleviate the otherwise sex-distracting element which is generally present at mixed retreats at other Dharma centres. Retreats, which can last from one week to a month, are usually well attended and are quite intensive with the emphasis on the evolution of the individual, both mentally and spiritually. All meals are vegetarian and an overall atmosphere of mindfulness of self and others is required. The retreats generally commence on Fridays and terminate on subsequent Saturdays. As with most retreats, early booking is advised so as to avoid disappointment.

The FWBO London, Mandala and Ratnadvipa

The FWBO movement in London has probably changed so much in the past couple of years that an up-to-the-minute account is likely to be ancient history before 1980. There have been so many comings and goings with the movement in London, that a disconnected assessment of the present situation is all that an outsider can aim at.

Up until December 1977, all the main activities and developments revolved around Pundarika in Archway. These consisted of meditation and Yoga sessions, karate classes, Dharma study groups and lectures and courses in human communication. Day retreats and seminars were also a characteristic of the 'early days'. Since its demise, however, all the north and west London areas have derived their stimulus from Mandala in Fulham. At present the Centre is running courses at Swiss Cottage in Hatha Yoga, with beginners' classes on Mondays and Meditation classes on Thursdays – *free of charge*. So far much enthusiasm has been shown by the public that an established centre at Swiss Cottage is proving a distinct possibility.

An added dimension to Mandala is its men's community in North London, the 'Jewel Island' Community called Ratnadvipa, whose present location is near the old Pundarika centre. The community has formed a Housing Association and hope to buy a house in west London soon. Ratnadvipa's Right Livelihood activities are many which include a removals business and an industrial co-operative, the Raft Co-op.

Mandala itself was formed in April 1976 as the F W B O West London and previously existed at the Friends Meeting House in Ealing. There are presently three Order Members associated with Mandala and a few Order Members from Sukhavati functioning as visiting teachers. Also associated with Mandala are several male and female Mitras who help out in the Centre's Right Livelihood activities.

Sukhavati

Sukhavati is the east London branch of the F W B O and is the largest of all the movement's communities throughout Britain. The Centre, which was previously an old fire station in Roman Road, Bethnel Green, has been undergoing renovation and conversion since the autumn of 1975. Over the past three years, work has been sporadic with the dwindling of funds – a problem which has since been overcome with the help of a grant from the Manpower Services Commission.

The community currently comprises thirty men, eighteen of whom are Order Members. The Order Members at Sukhavati meditate twice a day as well as performing Puja and organizing study groups. All Order Members are engaged in full-time work on the building as well as its Right Livelihood activities. These include a printing business, a wholefoods and retail business along with a transport and removals business.

All the above ventures take place under the general heading of the Pure Land Co-operative, who briefly are 'each committed to communicating as freely and openly as possible especially with those who share our commitment and feel due appreciation for all those who are sincerely making an effort to evolve'.

Down the road from Sukhavati is the East End Meditation Centre which recently came into existence and acts as the public centre for F W B O activities in east London. Beginners' meditation classes, courses in meditation and Buddhism, retreats and Yoga classes all take place here under experienced

Order Members. Situated directly above the Centre is the Golgonooza Community and the Windhorse Design Studios, both of which appear in a separate section of their own.

Sukhavati is the name given to Buddha Amitabha's Pure Land, or Western Paradise. In Shin Buddhism, according to Honen, those sincere devotees who faithfully repeat the mantra 'NAMU – AMIDA – BUTUS', go directly to Sukhavati where attainment of Nirvana is guaranteed.

Golgonooza

Golgonooza, or 'City of Art', is the FWBO's creative arts centre situated at 119 Roman Road. The centre is a more 'worldly' focus point than other centres with the emphasis on the arts and theatre.

Two Upasakas, Luvah and Siddhiratna, initiated the Golgonooza Association which comprises the Windhorse Design Studios and the Golden Drum Theatre Group. Windhorse Designs began by producing *Mitrata*, the movement's spiritual manual based on Bhante's lectures and seminars. The studio is engaged in the production of silkscreen prints, visual aids and a new edition of *The Three Jewels* by Bhante.

The Golden Drum Theatre Group is the other half of Golgonooza's creative arts foundation. A striking feature of the Group's repertoire is it's preoccupation with the works of Blake. The word Golgonooza comes from one of Blake's most famous poems *Milton*. All the casts involved in the Group's productions are Order Members and Mitras. The plays performed are not to be considered as straight acting roles for the performers, but as a vibrant vehicle for self-expression and communication. To expand beyond the purely aesthetic into the realms of spirituality is a trite definition of the thinking behind Golgonooza.

Aryatara

The movement's community at Aryatara is located at 3 Plough Lane, Purley and has been the central axis for FWBO activities in Surrey for nine years. In the early days the house catered for a mixed community and private study was most encouraged. But three years ago the format rapidly changed when more and more people were being attracted to the Buddhadharma. Meditation and Hatha Yoga classes developed, with the emphasis on public involvement and commitment. The Centre consequently became a registered charity and at this point was catering for about 150 to 200 people per week. Most of the income to support the Centre was derived from week-end and week retreats and this facility was extended to local Friends and F W B O centres in London.

However, in the past eighteen months, developments in the area have been further increased. Firstly, four Order Members joined the community which tended to increase the potential of their public activities. Secondly, after deciding to pool their resources together, a 'workers' co-operative' was established where community members received free board and lodgings, and were paid £5.00 per week pocket money. This led to the formation of two Right Livelihood projects, Rainbow Transport and Rainbow Decorating. Apart from providing the community with financial stability, this, alongside gifts and loans from other Friends, enabled the community to realize their ambition to establish a wholefood shop in Croydon.

After renting premises at St Michael's Road, Croydon in February 1978, the movement opened their wholefood shop five weeks later and named it 'Friends Foods'. The garden directly behind the shop was, in May, opened as a vegetarian café and called the 'Secret Garden'. This provided a focus point for Friends and Order Members to establish contact with the public on 'neutral' ground. The two floors above the shop provided the movement with yet another small community for four men, the whole complex coming under the general title of 'Kalpadruma', the 'wish-fulling tree.'

The latest episode to F W B O (Surrey) has led to fresh energy and an increase in the meditation, yoga and retreat programmes. It now leaves the movement with the next objectives of founding a women's community, expanding on the men's and

the possibility of the first family community within the
F W B O movement.

Aryatara has been an important centre for F W B O publications in the past and currently publishes a bi-monthly
newsletter called *Karuna*.

The women's communities

There are presently three women's communities within the
F W B O movement, all of which were founded in June 1977.
These communities function in a similar manner to the men's
communities, the only difference being that of gender. The
three are Amaravati and Beulah, both of London, and Mandarava of Norfolk.

Amaravati was founded in January of 1977 at a special winter
women's retreat. After negotiations with the Department of
the Environment, three Upasikas moved into the house at 30
Cambridge Park, London E11, after a long search for reasonably priced houses. Most of the people who moved into the
house had previously been associated with the Archway
Centre a few years earlier and were well orientated to communal life. After a year of renovating and decorating, the community have now got down to Right Livelihood activities.
Presently, the community are involved in their 'Kusa Cushions'
business which is being expanded to accommodate clothes,
upholstery and curtain-making.

On the spiritual side, the community meditate together in
the mornings and do Puja in the evenings. A weekly study
group, which includes a once-weekly taped lecture by Bhante,
forms the studious side of the community programme. The
community is also open to women visitors who wish to experience communal life as carried out in the F W B O, considering they pay their way and help out in the chores. At
present there is a community of five Upasikas which makes it
the largest women's community within the movement.

'Mandarava' is the women's community situated in the small
village of Aslacton, fourteen miles south of Norwich. Apart

from the community side, it also operates as a retreat centre for women. Mandarava is actually a three-storey farmhouse with outhouses, barns and greenhouses which, it is hoped, will eventually provide the community with the resources to become self-supporting in the future. The community also acts as a retreat centre; although retreats have been few owing to the volume of work needing done. It is hoped that in the future the community will concentrate on study seminars and retreats.

Beulah, the other women's community in London, is situated at Bishop's Way, E8, not far from Sukhavati. The community was formed by one Upasika and two Mitras and has since expanded to three Mitras and two Friends. It was deliberately set up for women who wished to lead a spiritual life in a community as well as holding down a full-time job. The community, therefore, does not cater for publicized functions or activities of any kind. Being near to Sukhavati and the East End Meditation Centre tends to attract Order Members and Mitras for discussions and tea, etc. The community is unlikely to alter this format in the future.

Addenda

The FWBO has characteristically not restricted its spread to Britain but has developed and founded centres and communities in other parts of the world. There are currently one centre in Finland, three centres and four communities (two mixed and two for men) in New Zealand, and a centre has already been established in India. This leaves the FWBO as the only British Buddhist organization to have founded centres beyond its own shores.

'FWBO Publications' is the movement's publications centre. Below is a list of books by Ven. Sangharakshita, some of which are published by FWBO Publications:

A Survey of Buddhism, Indian Institute of World Culture, 1957
The Three Jewels, Rider, 1967

The Essence of Zen, FWBO, 1973
Mind – Reactive and Creative, FWBO, 1974
The Path of the Inner Life, FWBO, 1975
Crossing the Stream, FWBO, 1976
The Thousand-Petalled Lotus, Heinemann, 1976
Sayings, Poems, Reflections, FWBO, 1976

7 The Zen Buddhist Priesthood — Throssel Hole Priory

The Soto Zen Priory of Throssel Hole

The journey to the temple has always been regarded as incredibly important because at that time you have no visible discipline from the temple. You are doing something about yourself by just going there. That is the first chapter of the Shushogi.* There is something I've got to do about me; I've got to understand life and death; I must go to the temple. So, no matter how far you may travel, the first real ceremony is the journey.

ROSHI JIYU KENNETT

I arrived at Hexham train station on a clear but coldish night during the early summer of 1973, having made previous arrangements to meet someone who would hopefully pick me up at the station and transport me to Throssel Hole Priory. This 'someone', I was not sure about, whether it would be a layman or priest I did not know. If it was a layman, I knew within myself that I could handle the situation – but a Zen priest – well I was honestly baffled. One had visions of a discreet, Bodhi-dharma-like monster wielding his kyosaku in a stoic attitude of indifference. Never having been near a Zen monastery before, I became excessively nervous at the immediate prospects of a week of sesshin – my first taste of Zen training.

*One of the teachings of the great Zen Master Dogen Zenji which deals with the true meaning of Enlightenment, and the training necessary to realize that state.

After about a one-hour-long wait and a constant surveillance of every vehicle that pulled up at the station entrance, I noticed a tall, black-robed figure emerge from a beaten-up old Austin Cambridge. I immediately realized that here was my 'chauffeur' and made my way to his side. The bristly headed monk, whom I later found out was Canadian, was the absolute opposite of the 'monster' I had formerly imagined. After all, Zen priests are a relatively new phenomenon on the British Buddhist scene.

On our journey to the Priory, Dogo related to me that he was the current Chief Junior and all the responsibilities that the post entails (I later discovered that a monk's term as the Chief Junior is probably the most trying of his first five years of training). Within an hour or so we finally arrived at the Priory. Unfortunately, the visitors had just bedded down for the night in the Zendo, so I didn't get a clear appreciation of my surroundings, only the exquisite fragrance of frankincense. What I did sense on my first night at the Priory was the un-mistakable aura of drama which prevailed. However, more of the sesshin in the latter half of this chapter. What is Throssel Hole and to whom or what does it owe its existence?

The Priory was founded by Roshi Jiyu Kennett in June of 1972 and is the sister centre to Shasta Abbey in California in which Roshi is the Abbess. Roshi was born in 1924 in England and showed in her earlier schooling a willingness to learn that continued with her study of music and later graduated B Mus., Durham University. This love of music saw her attain a Fellow-ship of Trinity College in London. Like many of her contem-poraries, she discovered the beautiful doctrine of Buddhism which was becoming more and more popular, especially with the young intellectuals of the day. Of course at that time Theraveda Buddhism was the principal school although there were several books and articles circulating in London which enumerated the Mahayana schools of China and Japan – not forgetting that Brilliant Buddhist scholar D. T. Suzuki.

During those early years, Roshi Jiyu Kennett joined, and subsequently lectured at the Buddhist Society. But later on she had a chance meeting with Suzuki who greatly impressed her and it was at this time that the Zen seed was planted. One of the most important events to take place in her life was her meeting with Rev. Chisan Koho Zenji, Chief Abbot of Sojiji Temple in Japan whom she arranged accommodation for on one of his rare lecture visits to the West. It transpired that he invited her out to Japan to become his disciple upon which she accepted. On her way out to Japan, she stopped off in Malaysia where she subsequently underwent ordination into the Chinese Rinzai tradition prior to moving on to Japan. Her early years at Dai Hon Zan Sojiji Temple were difficult but enlightening and the hard work proved efficacious with her appointment to Foreign Guestmaster. In this distinctive post, she was responsible for the training of Western Zen devotees.

The loyalty shown to her master and the profound understanding of Zen led her master to transmit the teachings as handed down by the Patriarchs, upon which she took control of Unpukuji Temple in Mie Perfecture. Whilst in Japan, she obtained the Sei Degree, roughly equivalent to our Doctor of Divinity, and was also named Roshi and granted a Sanzen licence.

In 1969, she returned to the West and set up 'home' in San Francisco where she founded the Zen Mission Society, whose objective was to disseminate the Soto teaching in America. This eventually led to the forming of Shasta Abbey, in an attempt to develop and train Westerners in the Soto Zen priesthood. Roshi, apart from her konastic commitments is an Instructor at the University of California Extension at Berkely and is on the faculty of the Californian Institute of Transpersonal Psychology.

In 1970, Roshi, accompanied by an American monk, and by invitation from several people, held two sesshins, one in London and the other in Gloucestershire. At these two sesshins a few people took lay-ordination (Jukai Tokudo), and the response was so enthusiastic that a permanent centre run on the same lines as that of Shasta Abbey, and sharing the same ideals as

Shasta was conceived and, in June of 1972, Throssel Hole was founded. This grew out of the British Zen Mission Society and became a registered place of worship.

Within a year of its inauguration, the Priory housed nine monks,* eight male, one female. Actually the Priory, a converted barn and farmhouse, was undergoing daily repair and visitors immediately realized that if they came to do serious training, then their stay would be, to say the least, austere. As Roshi said herself:

> Throssel Hole Priory is deliberately non-luxurious, but it is a lot more comfortable than the average Japanese temple. We are maintaining the spirit of Zen, at the same time expressing it in a British way.†

The central axis of the Priory is the Zendo which serves as accommodation for visitors, is the place where daily zazen is done and where all ceremonials and services are exercised. There is the usual shrine, and back in 1973 it consisted simply of a rupa of Kanzeon, the Bodhisattva of Compassion known also by his Sanskrit name of Avalokitesvara, and a couple of incense burners. Downstairs from the Zendo is the dining room where all meals are taken and the odd lecture over a cup of tea. The monks' quarters was the farmhouse itself which also contained the kitchen, an extremely important department of a Zen monastery.

The Priory had a slow start, as it were, possibly as the Zen tradition was to a certain extent overshadowed by the growing interest shown by the vast majority of British Buddhists in the Vajrayana Way of Tibetan Buddhism. Whatever the reason, I do not know, but in the middle half of 1973 the retreats and sesshins were becoming decidedly more attended and the increasing popularity of Throssel Hole spread. This growth was reinforced with the numbers taking Jukai Tokudo, ordinary men and women committing themselves to train for the

---

*The word monk is used here to denote both sexes.

† *Throssel Hole Priory Journal*, vol. 1, no. 1.

Enlightenment of self and all other sentient beings – with perhaps a little help from the great and kind Kanzeon.

Roshi spent the summer of 1973 at Throssel Hole and led many retreats and five successful sesshins during her stay. Throughout her period of residence, she emphasized the need for British Zen followers to remain British and to refrain from 'Oriental charlatanry'. Referring to the world-wide spread of Zen in recent times Roshi stresses:

Now Zen has come to England, and as when it went to America, it must hold no allegiance to Japan, but be its own master within its own country. It must grow and flourish, as did Zen in all other countries, and belong to Britain, albeit having connections all over the world. For we here in England need our own Buddhist identity.*

Because of this admonition, Throssel Hole has kept to Western ways of culture, e.g. eating with knife and fork – and not chopsticks, etc. Basically, and many people seem to forget this, that, it is the doctrine of Buddhism that has been handed down through the centuries and allowed to flourish, not the indigenous cultures.

In that same year it became increasingly obvious that the present site was entirely inefficient both in capacity and comfort. For instance, with a Jukai sesshin there could be as many as thirty visitors sleeping and meditating in the Zendo, a few requiring to use sleeping bags as there weren't enough beds to go round. It also became necessary to split the Zendo up into two sections, one for the men and one for the women, although sitting periods and ceremonials were done by all in an undivided Zendo. In order to improve the Priory's standards, an appeal went out to all friends and Zen Buddhists all over Britain to secure the funds for a new Zendo. Near the end of that year Roshi unfortunately had to return to the States and to her many responsibilities. However, before her departure she installed the new Prior and made an appeal for items to aid in the smooth running of the Priory as well as £2000 required to renovate the present buildings. This renovation

*Throssel Hole Priory Journal, vol. 1, no. 1.

work had been decreed by an architect who found that the main Zendo building was structurally unsound and, hence, the appeal. The problems met with the shortage of water were alleviated with the discovery of an underground water spring, the quality of the water being of an unusually high standard.

By the end of 1973, it was decided that a permanent building situated on the then car park site was the lasting solution to the new Zendo. Remarkably enough, money poured in in support of this new venture, £2500 to be precise, approximately half of the cost of the new building, which, it was agreed, would be built by themselves. The appeal for this money became rather urgent and I recall there being fears that the Priory would have to close unless the money was found, as the existing building was too dangerous to house any great number of visitors. Here was a recently established institution pledged to the training of Westerners in the Soto Zen tradition and finding itself on the brink of dissolution. This crisis was to last for another twelve months before planning permission was given. But on a more lighter note. In January 1974, the first Buddhist marriage was performed at the Priory and, as far as I know, was most successful.

The expansion of the Soto Zen tradition in Britain could be gauged by the growing number of affiliated Soto groups springing up all over the country. Here and there, small groups were opening their doors to isolated people who had attended Throssel Hole, and incidentally, to people who hadn't, to provide a service and a link with the Soto teaching. This has of course grown and now runs into some twenty groups. It was at this time that an establishment was formed called The London Zen Priory and was inhabited by three monks (all British), all affiliated with Throssel Hole, and served as a retreat for those wishing to meditate at a Soto Zen centre nearer the south of England.

By midsummer 1974, little or no progress had been made on the proposed new building which, it must be stressed, had to conform to the local planning office specifications. Amongst endless discussions with the architect and seemingly time-consuming assessments, a bit of good fortune was struck with the opening of a small coal pit which, it was hoped, would see the Priory self-sufficient in coal. As heating was a top priority at Throssel Hole, especially in the winter, it tended to lift the gloominess off an uncertain future. One piece of news which reached the Priory at this time was that Roshi would not be coming back to Britain that year as the commitment she had with Shasta Abbey was too taxing on her otherwise strenuous working and religious life. One of the questions being asked at this time was, when the time came, where would Roshi eventually settle down – Throssel Hole or Shasta Abbey? After all, she was getting on in years and even the most itinerant of teachers settled down sometime.

Between the summers of 1973 and 1974, the Priory experienced a coming and going of full-time monks and more and more people were becoming attracted to this particular and orderly way of life. Perhaps this was one of the best things that could be happening as the exploitation of the coal pit, the water spring, the ever-expanding 'animal farm' and the continual work of property restoration kept the monastic community very busy. Added to this was a quite serious religious life, sometimes hard and for the most part austere that combined to make a perfect Zen life. For it is said: 'No work – no food', and at the Priory this principle was observed passionately.

By the end of the year, the Priory was now offering a half a dozen week-long retreats interspersed with sesshins and weekend retreats throughout the year. Nearly every retreat was filled to capacity, a reflection of the level of training being undertaken. One new development which took place was that all new trainees wishing to become ordained would have to go through a three- to six-month postulant period prior to becoming a fully ordained Sangha members. Also two new ceremonials were added to the list of observances in the year, those being Segaki, or the ceremonial feeding of the hungry ghosts and the Founder's Day Ceremony dedicated to Rev. Keido Chisan Koho Zenji.

At the turn of the year, the Priory journal took on a more readable and tabloid form as well as an increase in the number of articles printed. This gave an ideal chance for anyone training in Soto Zen to air their view, or their frustrations, and it was heartening to see so many people committing themselves to the peerless and unending training of Zen. Here was the magnificent teaching of the Prajnaparamita – of 'always becoming Buddha in vast emptiness'.

By the summer of 1975, the aborted building programme finally got underway with the initial clearing of the old car park site. The only drawback encountered was the discovery of two small coal pits. This necessitated digging much deeper than originally planned and the filling of large cavities with rocks.

Probably the biggest disappointment of 1975, was the non-appearance of Roshi to the Priory, even although this was promised earlier in the year. Well, apart from the lack of funds to sponsor her trip, it would seem that she had an unusually busy year at Shasta which made her trip impossible. While still on the subject of money, you might wonder who sponsors the individual monks at the Priory. Well, the answer is that they are not sponsored as such. Each prospective monk finances his or her stay with money earned 'in the world'. This can take the form of say working for a year and saving the money in order to warrant possibly a year's residence at the Priory. If one really works at it, sacrificing many luxuries, even necessities, then one could take a trip to Shasta Abbey to train alongside many experienced Soto trainees.

The appeal launched in 1975 was most successful, with the accumulation of the necessary money within six months. Many supporters took out seven-year covenants, interest-free loans and some donated money from the sheer desire of seeing the Priory with a substantial building. As mentioned earlier, the coal pits which necessitated digging further than firstly anticipated, proved actually more beneficial to the foundations. Because of the old mines, and for safety's sake, a huge 150-ton concrete float was laid to make the Zendo's foundations unshakable. However, be that as it may, there was still a mountain of work to be done and plenty of cash required before the building work could begin.

In autumn of 1976, a new Prior was installed at the Priory, an American monk who had been a close disciple of Roshi at Shasta Abbey. The brick-laying had just begun on the new Zendo and evident progress was at last being made – the first time in twelve months. But no sooner had the work commenced when the Priory had to face another blow. The owner of the Priory grounds put it up for sale with an asking price of £10,000, an immense burden on an already tight budget. Immediately another appeal was launched to raise the necessary money in an attempt to avoid total disaster. But once again the Priory's friends stood loyal to the cause and the money flowed in to secure the grounds. At last the Priory was one unit and in the summer of 1977, the Charity Commission approved Throssel Hole Priory as a Charitable Trust.

A couple of months earlier, however, another development took place in the light of the fact that Roshi couldn't be with her British priests as much as she would wish. Hence, a decision was taken to temporarily move the monastic training of the monks from Throssel Hole to Mount Shasta. This would have the dual effect of allowing British priests to train under the direct guidance of Roshi, and the experience gained by training alongside some of Roshi's highly trained priests would prove extremely precious. It anything it would seem that when the priests return from Shasta after a few years with Roshi, it will undoubtedly enhance and refresh the whole Soto Zen movement in Britain.

At present the Priory is functioning as a retreat centre for sincere Buddhists dutifully administered by the Rev. Abbess.

Zen, extraordinarily enough, has taken some time to establish itself in Britain – and I not only refer to the Soto school. The Buddhist Society's Rinzai Zen classes are most popular and have been going for some years now under the guidance of Mr Christmas Humphreys and Irmgard Schloegl. Modern historical and cultural trends seem to be reflecting those of America, a phenomenon which can be witnessed by the growing number of 'New Age' truth-seekers which have emerged in Britain over the past ten years.

Nevertheless, the Dharma has established itself at Throssel Hole Priory due initially to Roshi Jiyu Kennett, and latterly, to the many adherents of the Soto Zen school. When the monks return from their studies with Roshi in America, the monastic institution of Zen Buddhism will once again be irrefragable in Britain.

Ceremonials and services in the Soto Zen way

Being basically a Zen training monastery, Throssel Hole provides a service to the layman and laywoman who wish to study and practise Zen Buddhism either in a monastic or lay-trainee capacity. Because of this, when one visits the Priory, whether it be on retreat or introductory visit, one participates in all the relevant services and sitting periods. However, some might have illusions about the Priory because of the Zen 'tag' which has unfortunately been pinned on it over the past ten years. Let us clear away this cloudiness from this beautiful way of life before progressing any further.

Zen Buddhism is, I feel, the most misunderstood way of mind training in the history of comparative religion. Its basic doctrine defies definition, at least in the rational sense, and any metaphysical speculations will prove utterly ridiculous as it cannot be grasped or packaged in small, neat bundles – if it could, then it would not be Zen. Roshi Jiyu Kennett explains:

> The main teaching of the Soto school that Dogen brought with him was that no words or scriptural text can adequately express the Spirit of Buddhism and therefore those who are bound by such words and scriptures can understand nothing of the Truth which had been Transmitted by the Buddha himself to his first disciple, Makakashyo, who had in his turn handed it on, from mind to mind down the line of patriarchs and disciples to the present day.*

Zen is Eternal Life, p. 96.

I think we in the West tend to be too chimerical about Zen, rather than getting down to the only way to know Zen – and that means to live Zen through the practice of zazen. Running to far and dusty lands will only create disillusion and perplexity if we think that the only way to experience 'real' Zen is to go to the country of its birth. As the Very Reverend Keido Chisan Koho Zenji concluded:

When the West is ready, it will find for itself its true teacher. That person may have learned in Japan, but he or she will definitely be one of their own nation and not a foreigner to them. So long as they want a Japanese teacher, they will never understand Buddhism, for they are in duality in so far as they are seeing Japanese and foreigners as separate in the Buddha Nature instead of one.*

When the Buddha Shakyamuni held up the flower and smiled at Makakashyo, he intentionally transmitted a mysterious teaching independent of word and letter and to this day has been handed down from master to disciple – eighty-three times! This unbroken lineage of patriarchs came down to Roshi's master Rev. Chisan Koho Zenji and continues. This teaching is the undisputable centre of Zen and it is the penetration of this teaching in the form of kensho (the enlightenment experience, to see into one's Buddha Nature) that gives Zen its especial flavour.

Obviously, with a little reading in Zen, the reader will doubtless realize that Zen can become frustratingly paradoxical, but Dogen translates in plain words:

When one studies Buddhism one studies oneself; when one studies oneself one forgets oneself; when one forgets oneself one is enlightened by everything and this very enlightenment breaks the bonds of clinging to both body and mind not only for oneself but for all beings as well. If the enlightenment is True, it wipes out even clinging to enlightenment, and therefore it is imperative that we return to, and live in, the world of ordinary men.†

---

*Ibid., p. xxx, introduction.
†Ibid., 'The Teachings of Dogen Zenji', p. 172.

At the Priory one is taught Soto Zen as handed down over the centuries by the patriarchs since Dogen himself. This takes the form of training in morality, devotion and zazen. By morality I mean the observance of the Three Pure Precepts and the Ten Great Precepts. By devotion I mean the development of the Heart of Kanzeon or the cultivation of a kind and compassionate attitude towards all men. And lastly, the practice of zazen as expounded in Digen's Fukanzazenji. To begin this three-fold training is the fountainhead of the Zen life. To live in the present – simply and without any expectations of fame and gain could be said to be the practical application of this fountainhead in everyday life.

An important aspect of the Zen life is the sesshin, the week-long period of meditation in the Priory, where manual work is cut down to a minimum and seated meditation is increased. To attend a sesshin is an unforgettable experience because, in many instances, one is forced to face oneself and one's life in its naked simplicity, and not as we would *like* it to be. Through the power of zazen, the contrivances we conjure up in avoiding the present moment become strikingly conspicuous.

I attended my first sesshin five years ago in 1973 at Throssel Hole and was probably the most inspiring week of self-discovery I have ever experienced. However, it should be understood, that one's experiences at sesshin should only be assessed from the point of view of a deepening progression in zazen and the embracing of the precepts.

The Priory schedules at sesshin, as I recall, has six periods of sitting, one period of kinhin,* two services, two lectures and three square meals per day (vegetarian), The day was broken up into integrated periods of zazen, lectures and work, to the point where one felt that the whole day was virtually one long meditation session. All meals were taken in the dining room, and in silence, being preceded by short ceremonials with the accent on showing gratitude to the provision of food and to each other by performing gassho.†

*Literally, walking mindfuness.
†See Glossary.

To advance in the Zen life, one must, whether living in the monastery or in the home, look upon life's drama as one's meditation. If zazen is confined to one sitting in the morning or evening, with nothing in between, then one's training will be drastically and unnecessarily limited. The integration of work and training is of supreme importance because the Buddha Nature is as immaculate in the drudgery of our working life as it is in the crystal clear luminosity of seated zazen. The sesshin combines these two elements until discrimination ceases – our work literally becomes our meditation and meditation our work.

As with the non-retreat schedule, the Priory's residents attend two ceremonies, the morning one devoted to the recitation of scriptures by Sekito Kisen and Tozan Ryokai, the evening service being the recitation of Dogen's celebrated Fukanzazengi or Zazen Rules. These recitations are augmented by the intermittent striking of the inkin* and are designed more as a meditation in themselves than a purely mechanical trimming.

With the presence of Roshi herself, the sesshin was naturally enough 'packed out' with little or no room for further meditators. During that particular sesshin, Roshi expounded on the role of the Chief Cook in the monastery as explained in the Tenzokyokan (Instructions to the Chief Cook) by Dogen. The kitchen, according to Dogen, is a place in the monastery where the monk aspires to cleanse his heart of all impurities, analogous with the separation of the sand from the rice.

Whilst at the sesshin, another important element was sanzen, the master–pupil interview where one relates one's particular problems, spiritual or religious. Of course in the Rinzai tradition sanzen takes the form of a mondo, a question/answer period where the master tests the pupil's understanding or penetration of the koan. But the most vital aspect of sesshin is zazen, the harmonization of body and mind in perfect, utter peace. Zazen, being a method of inner searching, requires of us great diligence

*See Glossary.

and assiduity. Dogen's injunctions of the thirteenth century rings true today as it did then:

> Do not discuss the wise and the ignorant. There is only one thing: to train hard, for this is true enlightenment. Training and enlightenment are naturally undefiled. To live by Zen is the same as to live an ordinary daily life.*

Perfect sitting is perfect enlightenment, but how many people can sit with a pure and undefiled mind at that. To be able to sit with a pure mind requires us to be extremely ethical minded. Being human with all its shortcomings, we find it difficult to lead a naturally moral life, hence the Precepts. To keep the Precepts, is to train our minds and to accept things 'as they are', to see ourselves and our surroundings in true perspective. To admit to our past inadequacy is to do Sange, a form of contrition. In admitting to our past mistakes, we allow ourselves to be open in the hope that by so doing we cultivate an honourable disposition towards everyone. At the Priory, one can take refuge and the subsequent embracing of the Precepts. Briefly, these are: do not kill; do not steal; do not covet; do not say that which is untrue; do not sell the wine of delusion; do not speak against others; do not be proud of yourself and devalue others; do not be mean in giving either Dharma or wealth; do not be angry; and do not defame the Three Treasures. It is not my station to commentate on the Precepts – only to try and live by them, but if the reader wishes further advice he should scan the Kyojukaimon by Keizan Zenji as it appears in Kennett Roshi's *Zen is Eternal Life* for a full and excellent explanation of the 'giving and receiving of the teachings of the precepts'.

Finally, I would like to conclude this chapter by quoting from Dogen's brilliant Bendoho or, 'How to train in Buddhism':

> The correct ordering of daily life is therefore the heart of Buddhism. When, by the correct ordering of our daily life, we exhibit

Zen is Eternal Life, p. 290.

the heart of Buddhism we are free from delusive body and mind. As this is so the disciplined life of the trainee is the embodiment of both enlightenment and practice, pure and immaculate since before time began. It is the first appearance of the koan. For those who follow it there is never any need to try and grasp enlightenment.*

★Zen is Eternal Life, p. 113.

8   Useful Information

A Pali/Sanskrit/Japanese glossary

Abbreviations
J Japanese
P Pali
S Sanskrit

Abhidhamma P: One of the 'three baskets' of the Buddhist Pitaka of the Theravada canon. The higher teaching of the Buddha containing a complete compendium of psychology, philosophy and mind-training.

Alayavijnana S: The spiritual and mental 'house', or Store-consciousness. This term implies a consciousness in which all the momentary and involuntary reflexes are stored and where the seed of enlightenment dwells.

Amida J: *See under* Amitabha.

Amitabha S: A Buddha of Compassion who resides in the Western Paradise. Amidists believe that the fervent and faithful calling of the name of Amitabha will secure them re-birth in the 'Pure Land'.

Anatta P: 'No-Soul', one of the 'three signs' of all conditional phenomena. A direct antithesis of the Atman in Hinduism.

Anicca P: Usually rendered as Impermanence. The fleeting and transitory nature of all existence.

Arhat S: Literally, a 'worthy one'. One who has strived through relentless self-effort to the goal of Nibbana.

Asavas P: The 'outflows' of sense desires, attachment to material and mental planes of existence, wrong views and ignorance.

G

Asoka s: King of Magadha (*c.* 270 BC). The great Buddhist ruler of India under whose reign Buddhism and Buddhist art flourished. As stated in the *Mahavamsa*, Asoka's daughter Sanghamitta took a branch of the original Bodhi Tree to Ceylon.

Asura s: These are fighting demons who reside in one of the lokas, one of the realms of rebirth.

Avijja P: Literally, not-knowingness. That which causes beings to cling to the endless round of re-births.

Baso J: Ma-tsu Tao-i (709–80). A Chinese Zen Master.

Bhikkhu P: A member of the Sangha. Originally a homeless wanderer or one who has gone forth into homelessness. A mendicant monk.

Bimbisara s: King of Magadha during the life and Enlightenment of Gautama.

Bodhi s: The enlightening principle, the result of perfect wisdom.

Bodhidharma s: The first Patriarch of Chinese Zen. The Indian monk who after embracing Buddhism travelled to China where, it is said, he sat facing a wall for nine years.

Bodhisattva s: One very close to Buddhahood but who renounces eternal Nirvana until 'every blade of grass is enlightened'.

Bompu Zen J: A form of sitting utilized for its physical advantages.

Bonten J: One of the four meditative planes in the Rupadhatu, or the world of form.

Bosatsu J: The Japanese term for a Bodhisattva.

Brahma s: The God-head of the Trimurti or Hindu Trinity.

Brahma Vihara P: The 'Four Divine Abodes'. See under Metta, Karuna, Mudita and Upekkha.

Buddha s and P: Historically, Gautama the man who attained Buddhahood and Founder of a world religion.

Buddhaghosa s: The fifth-century Indian Buddhist commentator. Renowned for his voluminous work the *Vissudhimagga* (*Path of Purification*).

Buddhi s: A faculty of understanding sometimes given as an intuition of Reality.

Butsuden J: In a Zen temple, the main Buddha hall usually enshrining the image or Rupa-Buddha.

Dai-funshin J: Illimitable perseverence or strength of purpose.

Dai-gidan J: The Great Doubt; An essential experience in the Koan system or Rinzai Zen.

Daikan Eno J: Hui-neng (638–713), the Sixth Patriarch of Chinese Zen.

Dana P: Generosity. This is one of the three roots of good. A positive altruistic quality to be cultivated by the Buddhist.

Daruma J: The Japanese name given to the Indian monk Bodhi-dharma.

Dentoroku J: *The Transmission of the Lamp*, compiled by a Chinese scholar Tao-Yuan.

Deva S: A supernatural being possessing magical powers. Also, a heaven, or one of the six lokas.

Dharma S: The Doctrine of the Buddha. Can also be rendered as a truth, law or system.

Dharmakaya S: The Dharma Body; one of the three Bodies of the Buddha according to the Mahayanist Trikaya doctrine.

Dhatu S: Is that which bears its own characteristic, an element.

Dhyana S: Meditation. Also, jhanic absorbtion. The Japanese translation of this term is Zen, which it must be understood, is a comprehensive system in itself.

Dogen J: (c. 1200–1253). Studied Zen under Master Esai and later travelled to China where he took up zazen (quiet sitting) as the principle method of attaining Satori in the Soto school. After four years, returned to Japan to teach the Soto Zen way. His greatest work was probably the *Shobogenzo* (*The Eye of the True Law*).

Dosa P: Hatred.

Doshin J: The Fourth Chinese Zen Patriarch.

Dukkha P: Usually rendered as suffering, pain, disease and death. However, unsatisfactoriness comes closest to this difficult Pali term.

Eisai J: (1141–1215). The original founder of the Rinzai school of Zen in Japan. Also the originator of the Tea Ceremony.

Eka J: (Hui-k'e 487–593). The Second Patriarch of Chinese Zen, and also the disciple of Bodhidharma. It was said that he cut off his right arm as proof of his sincerity of purpose.

Engo, Kokugon J: A Chinese Zen Master. Was the disciple of Goso Hoyen.

Eshi J: (515–77). Hui-ssu, the Second Patriarch of the Chinese Tendai sect of Buddhism.

Fudo J: A manifestation of Vairocana; the personification of the dynamic will for Enlightenment.

Fugen J: A Bodhisattva usually shown in mandalas, etc., as seated on a white elephant. He represents Truth and Love.

Gaitan J: A meditation seat used in Japanese monasteries for new trainees and postulants.

Gassho J: The Japanese term for the placing of the hands together at the chest as an expression of gratitude. A salutatory bow.

Gatha P: A verse of four lines found in the Suttas.

Gedo Zen J: Meditative practices used solely for the attainment of supernatural powers.

Gijo J: A state of mental tension which is cultivated prior to the attainment of Satori.

Goi J: Five rungs of a ladder in Zen meditation based on the relativity of opposites as devised by Tozan Ryokai.

Gunin J: (Hung-jen, 601–674). The fifth Patriarch of Chinese Zen. Gunin, who lived at Obai transmitted the 'mindless' doctrine to Hui-neng.

Guru S: A highly enlightened teacher.

Haiku J: A form of Japanese poetry containing seventeen syllables of three lines, in which is expressed the mysterious and yet profoundly simple aspect of Buddha-nature in all things.

Hakuin Ekaku J: (1685–1768). The founder of the modern Rinzai Zen school. He recorded much of his experiences in his book *Orategama*. Also author of the famous poem, *The Song of Za-zen*.

Han J: A wooden block struck in Zen temples at various times during the day.

Hetu P: Usually rendered as a 'causal condition' in Abhidhammic psychology.

Himsa S: Wickedness or cruelty, the exact opposite of harmlessness and compassion.

Hinayana P: The Small or Lesser Vehicle of Salvation. This system promlugates the Arhat ideal for the individual salvation of human beings.

Hogen J: (885–958). Founder of the Hogen school of Chinese Zen. He renounced the method of beating and shouting by continuous repetition of the question to the student.

Hossen J: A question and answer session similar to Mondo which is designed to test the understanding of a monk about to be promoted to a higher level of office.

Hossu J: A fly whisk used for ceremonial purposes.

Hyakujyo Nehan J: (720–814). Also known as Pai-chang Nich-p'an. A Zen master of the Nangaku line. He was the author of the *Hyakujyoshingi*, a training manual for novice monks, possibly his most famous utterance: 'No work, no food.'

Ingen J: (1592–1673). Founder of the Obaku school.

Inkin J: A small bell used in various ceremonials.

Ino J: A Zen disciplinarian.

Isan J: (771–853). A Chinese Zen Master who was the disciple of Hyakujo. He founded the Igyo school of Zen.

Jhana P: An ecstatic absorption leading to direct knowledge of Reality. There are various levels of jhanic concentration beginning with the Form Spheres Rupaloka) and ending with the Formless Spheres (Arupaloka).

Jinshu J: (606–706). A disciple of Gunin. Jinshu, it is said, because of his attachment to erudition and knowledge, hindered him in his realization of Nirvana.

Jodo J: The Pure Land or the Western Paradise.

Joriki J: The cultivation of supernatural powers obtained through intense concentration.

Joshu Joshin J: (778–897). A Chinese Zen Master and disciple of Fugan. His fame resides in his baffling Koan known as 'Joshu's Mu'.

Jukai J: The receiving of the precepts.

Kalpa s: An inestimable period of time, an epoch.

Kancho J: A priest who superintends in a Rinzai monastery.

Kanzeon J: The Bodhisattva Avalokitesvara who is a personification of compassion. In Chinese known as Kuan-yin.

Karma s: The law of cause and effect or action and reaction. The result of wholesome or unwholesome moral actions. A corollary to this is the philosophy of Rebirth.

Karuna s: Compassion. The wish to have the sufferings of those around us removed. One of the Brahma-Viharas.

Kasina P: An artifact used in the promotion of concentration.

Kensho J: A sudden flash of 'seeing into one's nature' comparable with Satori.

Kilesa P: A defilement of moral standards.

Kinhin J: 'Mindful walking' as practised in both Soto and Rinzai schools, interspersed with meditation.

Koan J: A paradoxical utterance or conundrum given to the student by the Zen Master in order to jolt him out of relativistic answers to an unanswerable question.

Koun Ejo J: (1198–1280). A Soto Zen Master and a disciple of Dogen. He was also the author of the *Shobogenzo Zuimonki*, a compilation of the sayings and lectures of Dogen.

Kyosaku J: A stick used in some Zen temples as a means to inflict on the student to greater efforts. Also, a ward of sleepiness.

Lankavatara Sutra S: Said to be the words of the Buddha himself as delivered on the mountain of Lanka in Sri Lanka.

Lobha P: One of the Three Roots of Evil. Literally means to cling, to attach. In its ultimate sense, 'Greed' or 'Craving'. As the second Holy Truth of the cause of suffering.

Lokas S: Six realms of rebirth; Heaven, human world, asuras, the animal world, hungry ghosts and Hell. Our Karma directly affects which one of these we are reborn into.

Madhyamika S: The School of Nagarjuna, whose system relied on the *Prajnaparamita* doctrine.

Maha Maya S: The mother of Prince Gautama.

Mahayana S: The 'Great Vehicle' of the Northern School prevalent in North India, Nepal, Tibet, China, Japan and Mongolia.

Makyo J: Visions seen in deep meditation caused by incorrect breathing or physical discomfort. Hindrances to meditation.

Mantra S: A mystical invocation repeated as a means to increase concentration. Used extensively in the Vajrayana of Tibetan Buddhism.

Mara S: The Evil One. The tempter of Shakyamuni on the night of his Enlightenment.

Metta P: Loving-kindness, goodwill. One of the Brahma-Viharas. Metta is used in meditation to banish ill-will or aversion from one's mind. Its central feature is benevolence.

Miroku J: The Buddha to come; his Sanskrit name is Maitreya and is said to reside in the Tusita heaven.

Moha P: Delusion, stupidity or bewilderment. Moha is that which clouds the mind and keeps us from seeing ourselves and the world around us as they really are.

Monda J: A question-and-answer system in which a Zen master 'interrogates' his student to plumb the depth of his understanding.

Monju, or Manjusri J and S: The Bodhisattva of Wisdom, always shown holding the 'delusion-cutting sword'.

Mudita P: Sympathetic joy. Another Brahma-Vihara or 'Divine Abode' in which one cultivates the acquiescence in others' successes. It eliminates dislike or jealousy.

Mudra s: A symbolic gesture of the hand used in the Vajrayana.

Mumonkan J: The *Gateless Gate*, a collection of Koans compiled by Mumon Ekai in the thirteenth century.

Nagarjuna s: Indian Buddhist of the second century AD. He founded the Madhyamika School of Buddhism and is considered the fourteenth Ancestor in Zen Buddhism.

Namarupa P: In Abhidhammic philosophy, name and form.

Namo Buddhaya P: Homage to the Enlightened One.

Nembutsu J: The Shin Buddhists recitation of Amida's name: 'Na-mu-a-mi-da-bu-tsu'. *See under* 'Amitabha'.

Nibbana/Nirvana P and s: The goal of the Eight-fold Path. The supra-personal experience of ultimate Reality; the complete extinction of all desires and attachments that bind us to Samsara.

Nivarana P: The Five Hindrances to Nibbanic bliss; namely: sense desires, ill-will, sloth and torpor, restlessness and worry, doubts.

Nyojo Zenji J: (1163–1228). The Abbot of Tendozan in China. He was the Zen master who transmitted the mind-doctrine to Dogen.

Obaku J: In Chinese: Huang-Po (?–850). A Zen master and disciple of Hyakujo Ekai. His most famous treatise was *The Transmission of Mind*.

Paccekabuddha P: An enlightened being but who does not endeavour to teach others in order to save them from re-birth.

Parinirvana s: On his death, Buddha is said to have passed into Parinirvana (final extinction).

Paticcasumuppada P: The Law of Dependent Origination. The causal formula of the arising of conditions dependent on a twelve link inter-related chain, these are: ignorance; activities; rebirth consciousness; mind and matter; six sense-spheres; contact; feeling; craving; attachment; becoming; birth; decay and death.

Patimokkha P: The 'Fundamental Precepts'. The 227 rules that every bhikkhu must observe which promote moral virtue, sense control and right livelihood.

Prajna s: Wisdom; the highest transcendental knowledge gained by enlightenment.

Prajnapamita s: A group of Scriptures which constitutes the heart of the Mahayana tradition.

Rinzai J: In Chinese: Lin-chi L-hsuan (?–867). A Chinese Zen Master and disciple of Obaku, also, the founder of the Rinzai sect. His most famous work, which includes the essence of the Koan system is the *Rinzairoku*.

Roshi J: A title for a Zen Master. It is said that the title of Roshi cannot be conferred on one who has not experienced genuine Satori.

Rupa s and P: Body; matter as distinct from mind. According to Abhidhamma rupa springs from four sources; namely – Kamma, Citta (mind), Utu (seasonal phenomena) and Ahara (Food).

Ryokan J: A Zen poet.

Saddha P: Faith or devotion to the Dharma. This is not blind-faith but a trustful knowledge based on insight.

Sadhana P: Spiritual practice.

Saijo Zen J: A form of quiet sitting where all desire for enlightenment have been appeased. Sometimes referred to as 'shikan-taza'.

Sakadagami P: One of the four stages of Sainthood. It is said that when one has eradicated the fetters of Kamaraga (sense-desire) and Patigha (ill-will), he becomes a Sakadagami, or 'Once-Returner'.

Samadhi s: As one 'segment' of the Eightfold Path (Right Effort, Mindfulness, Concentration). One-pointedness of thought.

Samatha P: Tranquillity or serene meditation. Can be developed to produce jhanic absorbtion as a way to realize Nibbana.

Sammyakusambodai J: The total Enlightenment of a Buddha.

Samsara s: The continuing round of birth and death. Extends to the higher levels of life, and the hells below that of the human world.

Samurai J: A Japanese warrior who embraced the Bushido Code as a way of life.

Sangha s: The Order of Monks or Bhikkhus. One of the Threefold Refuge.

San-zen J: An interview between master and disciple.

Sati P: Mindfulness; as one stage of the Eightfold Path. Also, carefulness, heedfulness or awareness.

Satori J: In Zen, illumination, a seeing into one's true nature or Buddha-mind. Absolute unexpressible insight which is lost if one tries to define it in any way.

Segaki J: A ceremony held at Hallowe'en in which the hungry ghosts are fed.

Sekito Kisen J: Author of the *Sandokai* in which the relative and absolute are blended in complete unity.

Shin J: An offshoot of the Pure Land sect.

Shingon J: The second largest Buddhist sect in Japan. Founded in 806 by Kobo Daishi, the Shingon is based on the *Mahavairocana Sutra*.

Sila P: Buddhist morality; the ethical precepts that bhikkhus are required to observe. Pancha Sila is the lay-Buddhist code of morality.

Skandhas S: The five aggregates which constitute the so-called personality or 'self'; namely rupa (body), vedana (feelings), Samjna (perceptions), samskara (mental-states), Vijnana (consciousness).

Sotapanna P: Another stage of Sainthood. At this level the bhikkhi realizes Nibbana for the first time and is regarded as a Stream-winner. It is said of one that he will undergo at least another seven lifetimes.

Soto J: The Southern school of Chinese Zen. The name derives from two Chinese monks Tozan Ryokai and Sozan Honkaju, hence Soto. This sect uses quiet sitting or zazen to promote Satori.

Stupa S: A hemispherical mound in which is enshrined sacred relics of the Buddha or other saint.

Sumiye J: Japanese ink painting.

Sunya S: The Void; an early Hinayana philosophy later developed to the full in The Mahayana as depicting all dharmas in their 'suchness' or 'as-it-isness'.

Taiso J: A term meaning 'Great Patriarch'.

Tan J: The raised platform in the Zendo in which the monks sit in meditation.

Tanha P: Craving or desire. As one of the 'Three Roots of Evil', Tanha is the endless desire for material and mental pleasures.

Tathagatha S: 'He who has thus arrived': a Buddha; a designation used by the Buddha when referring to himself.

Tendai J: The school of Buddhism founded in China by Chigi (538–97), whose followers believe that their philosophy dates back to Nagarjuna himself.

Tengentsu J: A supernatural power.

Theravada P: The Way of the Elders. The southern school of Buddhism which propagates the Arahant ideal.

Tosotsuten J: A heaven where Bodhisattvas dwell prior to coming back to earth to help humanity struggle for Enlightenment.

Tozan Ryokai J: A Chinese Zen master (807–69) and disciple of Ungan. His first name went to the Forming of the Soto school.

Tusita s: See Tosotsuten.

Ummon Bunen J: (?–949), also known as Yun-men. A Chinese Zen Master, Ummon, a disciple of Seppo Gizon, is said to have gained Enlightenment after his master flung him through a gate, thus breaking his leg.

Umpan J: A gong in a Zen temple usually rung at mealtimes.

Unsui J: A postulant monk.

Upekkha P: Literally, means seeing with balanced mind or impartiality. An important quality in the development of insight.

Vairocana Buddha s: The Illuminated One. The central figure in the Kegon school.

Vajrasattva s: A Bodhisattva and Second Patriarch of the Shingon school.

Vedana P: Feeling; one of the 'Five Aggregates'. The sensations which arise when any of the five organs of sense come in contact with their respective sense objects.

Vimalakirti s: An Indian Buddhist considered a Bodhisattva and contemporary of Buddha.

Vinaya s: The rules of discipline of the Sangha.

Vipaka s: Can be called the fruits or results of our actions.

Vipassana P: A method of meditation aimed at producing insight, or seeing things as they truly are. Usually developed along with samatha.

Vissudhimagga P: The voluminous work (twenty-three chapters) of the great Indian Buddhist commentator Buddhagosha.

Yama P: Literally, that which destroys pain.

Yasodhara s: The wife of Buddha when still Prince Siddhartha Gautama.

Zazen J: Sitting meditation, as expounded in Dogen's *Fukanzazengi*.

Zen J: The Japanese translation of the Chinese Ch'an, which in turn is derived from the Sanskrit Dhyana (meditation).

Zendo J: The meditation hall in a Zen temple.

A Buddhist directory

Author's note

This Directory has taken some time to compile and it cannot be said to be exhaustive of *all* the various Buddhist organizations which are presently offering a service to the serious enquirer. I offer my apologies to those groups who have been omitted.

In aspiring to mirror the substantial groups, centres, and societies existing throughout the length and breadth of the country, it has been my firm intention to present only those groups which have endured for a considerable time and who are firmly established. The sheer volume of small Buddhist groups and societies that have subsisted for several months and then disbanded might testify to my omissions.

Under the section on universities I have included only those who have had Buddhist connections in the past and present. Those wishing to enquire about Buddhist activity at a university near them should write to the Secretary of the university concerned. It is not wise in a book such as this to quote names of secretaries of university Buddhist groups as these are constantly changing.

The British Buddhist Association,
57 Farringdon Road, London, E C I M 3 J B
01–242–5538
also Arama, 48 Crowndale Road, London N W I I T P

Contact: Mr A. Haviland-Nye at Farringdon Road, Ven. M. Vajiragnana at Crowndale Road
Theravadin – Buddhist educational body – meditation sessions – bookstall – Pali language and advanced Buddhist courses (see page 91) – membership

The British Kempo Yoga Association,
Hakurenji, 40 Deansway, London N2

Contact: Rev. Terry Dukes
Chinese Kempo – Kempo yoga classes in the form of Yui-Cha – a development within Shingon Buddhism – seminars – lectures – demonstrations – membership

The British Mahabodhi Society,
5 Heathfield Gardens, London W4 4JU
01–995–9493

Contact: Mr Russell Webb
Theravadin – associated with the London Buddhist Vihara – meditation sessions – retreats – correspondence course – library –
bookstall – *Buddhist Quarterly* journal – membership (see page 65).

The British Shingon Buddhist Association,
Hakurenji, 40 Deansway, London N2

Contact: Rev. Terry Dukes
Chinese Buddhist – membership and instruction in the mystical
doctrines of Shingon-Shu Kongoraiden-Ha Buddhism – seminars
– meditation – ritual-sutra study – *Flowing Star* journal

The Buddhist Centre,
Oaken Holt, Farmoor, Oxford OX2 9NL
Cumnor 2231 or 2244

Contact: The Secretary
Theravadin – retreat centre – resident bhikkhus – lectures – Vipassana courses – ceremonies – beautiful surroundings (see page 74)

The Buddhist Society,
58 Eccleston Square, London SW1 1PH
01–834–5858

Contact: The General Secretary
All schools – weekly classes in Zen and Beginner's class – Sesshin –
basic meditation class – study classes in Tibetan and Theravadin
Buddhism – open days – Buddha Day celebrations – long list of
liaison officers – library – Shrine Room – lecture hall – bookstall –
correspondence course – membership – *Middle Way* journal
– yearly summer school at High Leigh, Hoddesdon, Hertford-
shire (see page 49 for history)

The Buddhist Society of Manchester,
3 Grosvenor Square, Sale, Cheshire M33 1RW
061–973–7588

Contact: Miss Francis L. Parkinson
Theravadin – now active for twenty – hold open meetings and meditation every second Saturday of each month

The Buddhapadipa Temple,
14 Calonne Road, Wimbledon Parkside, London s w 1 9
01–946–1357

Contact: The Senior Incumbent or Mr Graham Duncan
Theravadin – periods of Puja and meditation – Dhamma lectures and discussions – Abhidhamma classes – Lay Buddhist Association (see page 87) – resident centre for Thai monks – bookstall – small reference library – Shrine Room (see page 84)

The Buddhist Union,
128 Westbourne Avenue, Hull h u 5 3 h z
Hull 492882

Contact: Judith T. Jackson (Secretary)
Theravadin – very active Buddhist group – membership – meetings – 'Reviews' – works with other Buddhist groups – send SAE for introductory literature

Cleveland Buddhist Society,
103 Overland Road, Park End, Middlesbrough

Contact: Mrs Joyce Shaw
All schools – fortnightly meetings – meditation – discussion – exchanges of literature – membership

Derby Buddhist Group,
2 Harcourt Street, Derby d e 1 1 p u

Contact: Mr Geoff Carpenter
Tibetan (Kagyudpa) – although Tibetan in origin, discusses all topics related to the higher consciousness – membership – meditation

Dharma House,
8 Radford Road, Lewisham, London s e 1 3
01–318–4699

Contact: Mr Michael Hughes
Zen (Soto) – Soto training centre – zazen classes – retreats – sesshins – many articles for sale – booklets – a future retreat centre to be established in Cornwall

Dorje Dzong,
47 Mardy Street, Grangetown, Cardiff, Wales CF1 7QU
0222–25656

Contact: Mr Leighton Cooke (Director)
Tibetan (Nyingmapa) – weekly meetings – Puja and seminars – retreats

Dundee Buddhist Group,
20 Forebank Road, Dundee

Contact: Mr Roy Truesdale (Secretary)
All schools – 'a Buddhist society in miniature' – membership – meditation – discussions – taped lectures – library – Shrine Room – visits to other Buddhist groups

Dyfed Buddhist Group,
Angel House, Milo, Llandybie, Dyfed SA18 3NJ

Contact: Mr Arthur Smith
All schools – small retreat centre – instruction in meditation – Shrine Room

Edinburgh Buddhist Society,
7 Bruntsfield Gardens, Edinburgh EH10 4DX

Contact: Morton E. Bryce
All schools – membership made up of Zen, Tibetan, Theravada and FWBO Buddhists – five meetings per month – meditation and Puja – sutra study – tape lectures – all welcome

English Buddhist Community,
Lower Flat, 21 West Street, Ventnor, Isle of Wight

Contact: Mr Dennis T. Sibley
All schools – committed to the furtherance of the Ideal of Enlightenment – meditation – discussions – retreats – the formation of

'The Allan Watts Foundation' – encourages creative arts and crafts – *Empty Vessel* journal

The Friends of the Western Buddhist Order★

F W B O Glasgow – Heruka,
13 Kelvinside Terrace South, Glasgow 20
041–946–2035

F W B O Manchester – Grdhakuta,
9 Aylcliffe Grove, Longsight, Manchester 13

F W B O Norwich – Vajradhatu and Vajrakula,
41a and 41b All Saints Green, Norwich, Norfolk

Mandarva,
Street Farm, The Street, Aslacton, Norwich, Norfolk
Tivetshall 344

Padmaloka,
Lesingham House, Surlingham, Norwich, Norfolk
Surlingham 310

F W B O Brighton – Amitayus,
19 George Street, Brighton, Sussex
0273–693–971

F W B O London – Mandala,
86d Telephone Place, Fulham, London s w 6
01–385–8637

Sukhavati,
51 Roman Road, Bethnal Green, London E2
01–981–1225

★See page 100 – contact in the first instance the Secretary of each Centre/Community for further information. For overseas centres, communities and overseas representatives, contact the Office of the Western Buddhist Order, Padmaloka Community, Norwich.

Amaravati,
30 Cambridge Park, London E I I 2PR
01–989–5083

Golgonooza,
119 Roman Road, Bethnal Green, London E2
01–981–5157

Beulah,
95 Bishop's Way, London E8

F W B O Purley – Aryatara,
3 Plough Lane, Purley, Surrey
01–660–2542

F W B O Croydon,
Kalpadruma, St Michael's Road, Croydon

Ratnadvipa,
22 Macroom Road, West Kilburn, London W9

F W B O Edinburgh,
12 Bruntsfield Gardens, Edinburgh EH I 0 4DX

Golden Rosary Hermitage,
11 Grenville Road, Lostwithiel, Cornwall PL22 0EP

Contact: Pema Yangchen (Secretary)
Tibetan (Nyingmapa) – daily meditation – rituals – Tibetan painting
and weaving – accommodation and instruction in Buddhist
philosophy and meditation – Sanskrit and Tibetan languages,
medicine and iconography

Hampstead Buddhist Vihara (Dhammapadipa),
131 Haverstock Hill, London NW3
01–722–2618

Contact: Mr Maurice Walshe
Theravadin – Buddhist meditation centre with long history – daily
meditation and instruction by bhikkhus – Puja – lectures – courses

– Shrine Room – retreats – works in conjunction with the English Sangha Trust (see page 101)

Isle of Wight Buddhist Society,
49 Argylle Street, Ryde, Isle of Wight

Contact: Mr Eric Gould (Secretary)
Theravadin – weekly meetings for discussing Buddhist philosophy – meditation classes – affiliated to Buddhist Society, London

Isolated Buddhist Group,
'Longfield', Cooksmill Green, Chelmsford CM1 3 3SJ
024–548–650

Contact: Mr Derek White
All schools – a unique group of isolated Buddhists communicating by tape, fills a much-needed service for those who by geographical isolation cannot meet fellow Buddhists.

Kagyu Samye-Ling Tibetan Centre,
Eskdalemuir, Langholm, Dumfriesshire, Scotland
Eskdalemuir 232

Contact: The Secretary
Tibetan (Kagyudpa) – Tibetan meditation and cultural centre – long- and short-term residence – meditation – Puja – crafts – Shrine Room – library – seminars – courses – retreats (see page 105 for history.)

Kampo Gangra Pema Ling,
Llwyncelyn, Crosswell, Crymych, Dyfed, Wales

Contact: Mr Roger Marshall
Tibetan (Kagyudpa) – a Kampo Gangra centre – meditation – Puja – week-end retreats – programme of seminars – tapes – Shrine – week-end courses

Kampo Gangra Kagyu Ling,
1a Reynard Road, Chorlton, Manchester 21
061–881–5221

Contact: Miss Angela Williams
Tibetan (Kagyudpa) – meditation and study centre – Puja – lectures – seminars – courses – introductory and advanced classes – week-end courses – accommodation – *Creative Space* journal

Karma Kagyu Cho-Ling,
28 Beaumont Rise, London N 1 9

Contact: The Secretary
Tibetan (Kagyudpa) – meditation and study centre – retreats – courses – seminars – Puja and meditation – Shrine Room – accommodation

Karma Ling,
49 Coventry Road, Market Harborough, Leicestershire

Contact: Mr Alex D. Wilding
Tibetan (Kagyudpa) – centre for Buddhist studies – Shrine Room – library – meditation – sutra study – Puja – retreats

Karma Naro Tibetan Buddhist Centre,
Middle Weanllt, Llanigon, Hay-on-Wye, Wales

Contact: Mr Kurt Schaffhauser
Tibetan (Kagyudpa) – meetings for Puja and week-end study groups

Kham Tibetan House,
Ashdon, Saffron Walden, Essex CB 10 2 HM
Ashdon 415

Contact: The Secretary
Tibetan (Kagyudpa) – meditation and retreat centre – lectures and seminars – long- and short-term residence – Shrine Room – library – courses (see page 115)

Kongoryuji,
29 London Road, East Dereham, Norfolk

Contact: Rev. Terry Dukes
Ch'an Buddhist – a new temple dealing in the meditational and theoretical aspects of the Shingon Mandala teachings and rites – more of a residential retreat for those wishing to devote long periods of time to meditation, etc.

The Lay Buddhist Association,
c/o The Buddhapadipa Temple, 14 Calonne Road, Wimbledon
Parkside, London s w 19
01–946–1357

Contact: Mr Graham Duncan (Secretary)
Theravadin – meditation – lectures – seminars – discussions –
membership – use of Temple – Buddha Day festival (see page
87)

The Liu Academy,
13 Gunnersbury Avenue, Ealing Common, London w 5
01–993–2549

Contact: Liu Hsiu-ch'i
Taoist and Ch'an Buddhist – educational and spiritual centre for
the study of Taoist therapeutics and Buddhist meditational
techniques – courses include Tai Chi Ch'uan, Chinese language,
Ch'an philosophy, Taoist music, calligraphy and I Ching studies –
open from 2 p.m.–9 p.m. weekdays and 10 a.m.–6 p.m. Sat.
and Sun.

London Buddhist Vihara,
5 Heathfield Gardens, London w 4 4 J u
01–995–9493

Contact: Mr Russell Webb
Theravadin (see under British Mahabodhi Society and pages 65–74)

London Zen Studies,
10 Belmont Street, London n w 1
01–485–9576

Contact: Mr Michael Shayer (Secretary)
Zen (Rinzai) – promotes the teachings of Sochu Suzuki Roshi –
daily zazen – zendo – sesshin – visit on Monday or Thursday
evenings

The Manjushri Institute,
Conishead Priory, Ulverston, Cumbria l a 12 9 q q
0229–54019

Contact: Mr Roy Tyson (Secretary)

Tibetan (Gelugpa) – residential centre for Tibetan Buddhism – long- and short-term residence – Shrine Room – meditation – seminars – retreats – Puja – courses – College of Tibetan Buddhist Studies – resident lamas and gelongs – many articles and books for sale (see pages 129–51)

Marpa Institute,
East Barton Road, Great Barton, Bury St Edmunds, Suffolk
028–487–388

Contact: Mr Chris Sladdin (Secretary)

Tibetan (Kagyudpa) – residential meditation and study centre – seminars – retreats – courses – meditation – Shrine Room – library

Mousehole Buddhist Group,
Penaluna, Clodgy Moor, Paul, Penzance, Cornwall TR19 6UR
0736–73–449

Contact: Mr Bill Picard

Zen – meditation group following the Zen tradition – zazen and discussion sessions – week-end and day retreats – non-residential – affiliated to the Buddhist Society, London – visiting speakers

North Staffs Zazen Group,
21 Longton Road, Stoke-on-Trent ST4 8ND
0782–657–851

Contact: Mr John Forse

Zen (Soto) – meetings for periods of zazen and kinhin – readings, discussions and tea – small library – affiliated to Throssel Hole Priory

Nottingham & District Buddhist Society,
26 Millicent Road, West Bridgeford, Nottingham

Contact: Mr Alan G. McCormick

All schools – weekly meetings for meditation – talks – sutra reading – taped lectures – liaison with other groups – help for beginners in Buddhism

Orgyen Cho-Ling,
76 Princess Street, London N W 6 5 Q X
01–624–8246

Contact: The Secretary
Tibetan (Nyingmapa) – Dharma centre in the tradition of Padmasambhava – meditation – Yoga and Tantra – seminars – week-end
   courses – three years' graduated course – Buddhist philosophy
   and psychology – Puja – limited accommodation – Shrine Room

The Pali Text Society,
62 South Lodge, Circus Road, London N W 8 9 E T

Contact: Miss I. B. Horner
Theravadin – an institution dealing with the translations and sales
   of the Pali Canon literature – (*not* a Dharma centre, purely an
   academic institution) – membership – book list (see pages 21–34
   for history)

The Pali Buddhist Review,
51 Wellesley Road, Ilford, Essex

Contact: Mr Russell Webb
Theravadin – a scholarly periodical published three times a year
   on Theravada Buddhism – covers topics taken from the Pali
   Canon itself – annual subscription – send S A E for details

Thinley Rinchen Ling,
8 Camden Terrace, Hotwells, Bristol B S 8 4 P U
0272–211620

Contact: The Secretary
Tibetan (Sakyapa) – first Sakyapa centre to be established in Britain
   – meditation and study centre emphasizing philosophical development and meditation practice – bi-monthly seminars – weekly
   meetings on Tuesdays and Fridays

Throssel Hole Priory,
Carr Shield, Hexham, Northumberland N E 47 8 A J L
049–85–204

Contact: The Guestmaster

Zen (Soto) – Zen Buddhist monastery following the Soto Way –
monastic and lay residence – daily zazen – ceremonials and
services – sesshin – week-end and introductory retreats – book sales
– *Throssel Hole Priory Journal* (annual subscription) – sanzen –
many associated groups (see pages 178–92)

The Tibet Society of the UK,
The Liberal Club, 1 Whitehall Place, London s w 1
01–930–1308

Contact: Ugyn Norbu

A non-political organization founded in 1959 to assist the Tibetan
cause in the West – membership – newsletter – many up-to-the-
minute reports and news on the exiled Tibetan Government
in India – many social activities – Tibetan Buddhist lectures and
seminars

Tyneside Zen Buddhist Association,
91 Chandler Court, Jesmond, Newcastle-upon-Tyne
0632–813752

Contact: Mr Robin Forrest

Zen (soto) – Zen Buddhist group associated with Throssel Hole
Priory and twenty other lesser groups – weekly meetings for
zazen and discussions – publish an interesting journal *Zen News*,
circulation approximate 200

The Vipassana Meditation Centre,
Chapter House, Gorefield Road, Leverington, Wisbech, Cam-
bridgeshire PE 1 5 5 AS
0945–3838

Contact: The Secretary

Theravadin – instruction and practice in Vipassana meditation –
one-week and two-week retreats – private interviews – two and
four months' residential accommodation – Shrine – book sales

West Midlands Centre for Mahayana Buddhism,
'Owls Roost', 38 Orton Avenue, Walmley, Sutton Coldfield
02 –351–1966

Contact: Mrs Rosina Eaton

Tibetan (Kagyudpa) – a Tibetan Buddhist centre following the teachings laid down in the Kagyu school – meditation – courses – membership – seminars – tapes – *Vayama* journal – in association with the Sutton Coldfield Buddhist Society (contact the same address)

The Wolverhampton Centre for Mahayana Buddhism,
567 Stafford Road, Fordhouses, Wolverhampton WV10 6QE

Contact: Mr William Giddings

Tibetan (Kagyudpa) and Zen – a twin centre following the Tibetan Vajrayana tradition of the Kagyudpa school – and the Seishin-shori-Ryu or 'Spirit Victory School' of the Zen-orientated Martial Arts Way.

Universities
The following universities have Buddhist activities.

Cambridge University Buddhist Society,
P1 Whewell's Court, Trinity College, Cambridge

Durham University Buddhist Society,
School of Oriental Studies, Elvet Hall, University of Durham, Durham

Hull University Buddhist Society,
Hull University Union, Hull, East Yorkshire

Lancaster University Buddhist Society,
Lonsdale College, Lancaster University, Bailrigg, Lancaster

Manchester University Buddhist Society,
46 Brailsford Road, Fallowfield, Manchester.

Nottingham University Buddhist Society,
Portland Building, The University, Nottingham

Oxford University Buddhist Society,
c/o Department of Experimental Psychology, South Parks Road, Oxford OX1 3PS

Bibliography

Abbreviations

PTS – Pali Text Society
BPS, Kandy – Buddhist Publications Society

Theravada Buddhism

The Book of the Kindred Sayings, Mrs T. W. Rhys Davids (2 volumes), PTS, 1917 and 1922
The Buddha and His Teachings, Narada Thera, BPS, Kandy, 1964
The Buddha's Ancient Path, Piyadassi Thera, BPS, Kandy
The Buddha's Way, Ven. Saddhatissa, Allen & Unwin
Buddhism in a Nutshell, Narada Thera, BPS, Kandy
A Buddhist Dictionary, Nyanatiloka Thera, BPS, Kandy
Buddhist Meditation, Edward Conze, Allen & Unwin, 1956
Buddhist Meditation in the Southern School, Constant Lounsbery
Cosmic Law in Ancient Thought, Prof. T. W. Rhys Davids, PTS, 1919
The Dhammapada, Narada Thera, WOE series, John Murray, 1954
Dimensions of Buddhist Thought, Francis Story, BPS, Kandy, 1976
Guide through the Abhidhamma Pitaka, Nyanatiloka Thera, BPS, Kandy
The Heart of Buddhist Meditation, Nyanaponika Thera, Rider, 1962
The Life of the Buddha, Nanamoli Thera, BPS, Kandy
Life of the Buddha, Ven. Saddhatissa, Allen & Unwin
A Manual of Abhidhamma, Narada Mahathera, BPS, Kandy
Manual of a Mystic, F. L. Woodward, PTS, 1916

The Middle Length Sayings (Majjhima-Nikaya) (3 volumes), Miss I. B. Horner, PTS, 1954, 1957 and 1959

Mindfulness of Breathing, Nanamoli Thera, BPS, Kandy

Pali-English Dictionary, edited by Prof. T. W. Rhys Davids and W. Stede

The Path of Purification, Nanamoli Thera, BPS, Kandy, 1975

Power of Mindfulness, Nyanaponika Thera, BPS, Kandy

Progress of Insight, Ven. Mahasi Sayadaw, BPS, Kandy

The Psychological Attitude of Early Buddhist Philosophy, Lama Anagarika Govinda, Rider, 1961

Re-birth as Doctrine and Experience, Francis Story, BPS, Kandy

Some Sayings of the Buddha, F. L. Woodward, Oxford University Press, 1925

The Thinker's Note Book, Bhikku Nanamoli, BPS, Kandy

The Way of Mindfulness, Soma Mahathera, BPS, Kandy

Way of Non-Attachment, Dhiravamsa, Turnstone, 1975

What the Buddha Taught, Walpola Rahula, Gordon Fraser

What Was the Original Gospel in Buddhism?, Mrs T. W. Rhys Davids, Home University Library

The Word of the Buddha, Nyanatiloka Mahathera, BPS, Kandy

Books on Tibetan Buddhism

The Buddhism of Tibet, L. A. Waddell, Heffer, 1939

Buddhism of Tibet/Key to the Middle Way, HH the Dalai Lama, Wisdom of Tibet series, no. 1, 1974

Creative Meditation and Multi-Dimensional Consciousness, Lama Govinda, Allen & Unwin, 1977

Cutting through Spiritual Materialism, Chogyam Trungpa, Robinson & Watkins, 1973

Dawn of Tantra, Chogyam Trungpa/H. Guenther, Shambala, 1975

Dharmas without Blame, Chogyam Trungpa, Shambala

Foundations of Mindfulness, Chogyam Trungpa, Shambala, 1976

Foundations of Tibetan Mysticism, Lama Govinda, Rider, 1960

Guide to the Jewel Island, Olshak/Wangyal

Hundred Thousand Songs of Milarepa, Garma C. C. Chang, Shambala, 1962

Initiations and Initiates in Tibet, Mme David Neel, Rider, 1931

Karmapa, Black Hat Lama of Tibet, N. Douglas, Louzac, 1976

Magic and Mystery in Tibet, Mme David Neel, Penguin, 1937

Mantras – Sacred Words of Power, J. Blofeld, Allen & Unwin, 1977

Mudra, Chogyam Trungpa, Shambala, 1972

Opening of the Wisdom Eye, HH the Dalai Lama, Social Science Ass. Press, Thailand, 1968

Peaks and Lamas, Marco Pallis, Woburn, 1974

Preliminary Practices of Tibetan Buddhism, Geshe Rabten, Library of Tibetan Works and Archives, 1977

Tantric Mysticism of Tibet, J. Blofeld, Dutton, 1970

Tantric View of Life, H. Guenther, Sanskrit Serres, Benares, 1952

Teachings of Tibetan Yoga, Garma C.C. Chang

Tibetan Book of the Dead, W. Y. Evans-Wentz, Oxford University Press

Tibetan Book of the Great Liberation, W. Y. Evans-Wentz, Oxford University Press

Tibetan Sacred Art – the Heritage of Tantra, D. Lauf, Shambala, 1976

Tibetan Yoga and Secret Doctrine, W. Y. Evans-Wentz, Oxford University Press

Tibet's Great Yogi Milarepa, W. Y. Evans-Wentz, Oxford University Press

Treasures on the Tibetan Middle Way, H. Guenther, Shambala, 1976

Visual Dharma, Chogyam Trungpa/H. Guenther, Shambala, 1975

The Way and the Mountain, Marco Pallis, Peter Owen

The Way of the White Clouds, Lama Govinda, Rider, 1966

Books on Zen Buddhism

Empty Mirror, Van de Wtering, Routledge & Kegan Paul, 1973

Essays in Zen Buddhism (3 volumes), D. T. Suzuki, Rider, 1949 and 1953

Fingers Pointing towards the Moon, Wei Wu Wei, Routledge & Kegan Paul

A First Zen Reader, Trevor Leggett, Tuttle, 1960

A Flower Does Not Talk, Zenkei Shibayama, Tuttle, 1970

Games Zen Masters Play, R. H. Blyth, Mentor

The Goose Is Out, W. J. Gabb, Buddhist Society, 1973

A History of Zen Buddhism, H. Dumoulin, Faber

Introduction to Zen Buddhism, D. T. Suzuki, Rider, 1949

Manual of Zen Buddhism, D. T. Suzuki, Rider, 1950

Mysticism, Christian and Buddhist, D. T. Suzuki, Allen & Unwin, 1971
On Having No Head, D. E. Harding, Buddhist Society, 1975
The Practice of Zen, Chen-chi Chang, Harper & Row
Studies in the Lankavatara Sutra, D. T. Suzuki, Routledge & Kegan Paul, 1930
Sutra of Hui-Neng, translated by Wong Mov-Lam, Luzac, 1944
The Way of Zen, Alan Watts, Penguin, 1962
Wisdom of the Zen Masters, Irmgard Schloegl, Sheldon
Zen – a Manual for Westerners, S. Sekiguchi
Zen and the Comic Spirit, M. C. Hyers, Rider, 1974
Zen and Zen Classics (5 volumes), R. H. Blyth, Hokuseido
Zen Buddhism, Christmas Humphreys, Heinemann, 1949
Zen Comes West, Christmas Humphreys, Allen & Unwin, 1953
Zen Comments on the Mumonkan, Z. Shibayama, Harper & Row, 1974
Zen Doctrine of No-Mind, D. T. Suzuki, Rider, 1949
Zen Flesh, Zen Bones, Paul Reps, Tuttle, 1957
Zen for the West, Sohaku Ogata, Greenwood, 1973
Zen in the Art of Archery, E. Herrigal, Pantheon, 1953
Zen Is Eternal Life, Jiyu-Kennett Roshi, Dharma, 1976
Zen Life, Koji Sato, Weatherhill, 1972
Zen Master Dogen, Yuho Yokoi, Weatherhill, 1976
Zen Mind, Beginner's Mind, Suzuki Roshi, Weatherhill, 1970
Zen Revival, Thomas Merton, Buddhist Society, 1971
Zen Teachings of Huang-Po, J. Blofeld, Grove, 1958
Zen Teachings of Hui Hai, J. Blofeld, Rider, 1970
Zen Teachings of Rinzai, Irmgard Schloegl, Sheldon
The Zen Way, Irmgard Schloegl, Sheldon, 1977

Anthologies and general

The Blue Cliff Records, translated by R. D. M. Shaw, Michael Joseph
Buddhism, Christmas Humphreys, Penguin, 1951
Buddhism in Translation, H. C. Warren, Harvard University Press, 1906
Buddhism – its Essence and Development, Edward Conze, Cassirer, 1953
Buddhist Bible, Dwight Goddard, Harrap, 1957

Buddhist Scriptures, Edward Conze, Penguin, 1959

Buddhist Texts through the Ages, Conze, Horner and Waley, Cassirer, 1954

The Buddhist Way of Life, Christmas Humphreys, Allen & Unwin, 1969

Cloud Hidden, Whereabouts Unknown, Alan Watts, Cape, 1974

The Creed of Buddha, E. G. Holmes, Greenwood, 1973

The Essence of Zen, Ven. Sangharakshita, F W B O, 1973

Gotama the Buddha, S. Radhakrishnan, Hind Kitabs, Bombay, 1945

Journey into Burmese Silence, Marie B. Byles, Allen & Unwin, 1962

The Light of Asia, Sir Edwin Arnold, Routledge & Kegan Paul, 1971

Lotus of the Wonderful Law, W. E. Soothill, Curzon, 1975

Precious Garland and Song of Four Mindfulnesses, Nagarjuna/7th Dalai Lama, Allen & Unwin, 1975

Secrets of the Lotus, D. K. Swearer, Macmillan, New York, 1971

Sun Buddhas, Moon Buddhas, Elsie Mitchell, Weatherhill, 1973

A Survey of Buddhism, Ven. Sangharakshita

The Teachings of the Compassionate Buddha, E. A. Burtt, Mentor, 1955

Theory and Practice of the Mandala, G. Tucci, Rider, 1961

This Is IT!, Alan Watts, Rider, 1978

Thousand-Petalled Lotus, Ven. Sangharakshita, Heinemann, 1976

Walk On!, Christmas Humphreys, Buddhist Society

The Wheel of Life, J. Blofeld, Rider, 1959

The Wisdom of Buddhism, edited by Christmas Humphreys, Rider, 1960

Zen Dictionary, Ernest Wood, Philosophical Library, New York, 1957

Index

Abhidhamma Pitaka, 23
Abhisamayalankara, 46
Acharn Cha, Ven., 103
Akong Tarap Rimpoche, Ven.,
    106, 110
Ananda Maitreya Mahathera,
    Ven., 77
Arnold, Sir Edwin, 37–9
Austin, Rev. Jack, 100
Avalokitesvara, 128

Bodhicaryavatara, 147
Born in Tibet, 106
British Buddhist Association, 24,
    91
    Basic Buddhism Course, 94–100
British Mahabodhi Society, 51
British Zen Mission, 181
Buddha, taking refuge in, 88
Buddha Dorje Chang, 116
Buddha Jayanti, 56, 68
Buddhapadipa Temple, The, 61, 84
    week-day schedule, 88
Buddhasasana Samagama, 44
Buddhism in England, 51–2, 161
Buddhist Centre, The (Oaken
    Holt), 74–84
    opening ceremony, 76
    Samanera Ordination, 82–4

'Buddhist Directory', 203–15
Buddhist Lodge, The, 49–51
Buddhist Publication Society,
    Kandy, 73
Buddhist Review, The, 44, 50
Buddhist Society, The, 48–64, 179
    associated groups, 64
    Diamond Jubilee, 58
Buddhist Society of Great Britain
    and Ireland, The, 18, 44, 49
Burnouf, E., 40

Chuang Tsu, 21
College of Tibetan Buddhist
    Studies, 130, 146
    details of courses, 150
Conze, Dr E., 56, 59
    biography and major
    publications, 45–8
Critical Pali Dictionary, 26
Crown Prince Tenzing Namgyal,
    115, 120–1

Dalai Lama, HH the, 61
    visit to the West, 151–9
DeZoysa, Sir Cyril, 67
Dhamma, 88
Dhammadatu bhikkhus, 84
Dhammapadipa, 101

Dhammasudhi, Chao Khun
    Sobhana, 86
Dharma Trust, The, 123
Dharmapala, Anagarika, 50–2,
    65–7, 74
Dialogues of the Buddha, 33
Dilgo Khentse Rimpoche, 123
Dogen, Zen Master, 178, 188, 191

Encyclopedia of Buddhism, 27
English Sangha Association, 102
English Sangha Trust, 102, 133
Essays in Zen Buddhism, 57

Fausboll, Victor, 30
Five Precepts, 101
Four Foundations, 124–6
Four Great Meditations, The, 142–4
Friends of the Western Buddhist
    Order (FWBO), 160–77
FWBO abroad, 176
FWBO communities and centres
    'Amaravati', 175
    'Amitayus', 167
    'Aryatara', 173
    'Beulah', 176
    'Golgonooza', 173
    'Heruka', 168
    'Mandala', 171
    'Mandarava', 175
    'Padmaloka', 170
    'Pundarika', 163
    'Ratnadvipa', 171
    'Sukhavati', 172
    'Vajradhatu', 169
    'Vajrakula', 169
FWBO network, 165–7

Gelugpa school of Tibetan
    Buddhism, 130
Geshe Rabten, Ven., 121, 132, 133
Great Prostrations, *see* Four
    Foundations

Hampstead Buddhist Vihara, 85,
    101, 162
Haviland-Nye, A., 72, 92
Hewavitarne, L., 70
Hibbert Lectures, 22, 28, 29
Horner, Miss I. B., 24, 62,
    71
Humphreys, Christmas, 51, 54, 59,
    61, 62, 71, 152, 186

Impermanence, *see* Four Great
    Meditations
India Society, The, 33

Johnstone House Meditation
    Centre, *see* Kagyu Samye-Ling
Jukai Sesshin, 182

Kagyu Samye-Ling, 104–8
Kagyudpa school of Tibetan
    Buddhism, 108
Kalff, Dr Dora, 137
Kapilavaddho, Bhikkhu, *see*
    Purfurst
Karma, *see* Four Great Meditations
Karmapa, HH the Gyalwa, 108,
    114, 115, 118, 122
Kham Tibetan House, 115–29
    Grand Opening, 120
    daily programme, 124
Kinhin, 189

Lama Chime Rimpoche, 61, 62,
    115, 116, 117, 118
Lama Je Tsongkapa Rimpoche,
    141–2
Lama Kalu Rimpoche, 122
Lama Thubten Yeshe, 132, 134,
    137
Lama Thubten Zopa, Rimpoche,
    132, 134, 135, 137
Lam.rim, 130, 140
Lam.rim Chen.mo, 149

Lay Buddhist Association, 85, 87
Legget, Trevor, 100
Library of Tibetan Works and
  Archives, 137
Light of Asia, The, 18, 38, 43
London Buddhist Vihara, 65

Madhyamikavatara, 148
Mahamudra, 108
Mandala Offering, The, *see* Four
  Foundations
Manjushri Institute, The, 129–51
Manual of Abhidhamma, A, 23
March, Arthur C., 57
Marpa Institute, The, 123,
Metteyya, Ananda, 18, 49
  biography, 43–5
Middle Way, The, 56, 58, 63,
  111
Muller, Max, 30
  biography, 39–41
Myat Saw, U, 75

Narada Thera, Ven., 68

Oldenburg, Herman, 30
'Om Mani Padme Hum', 129

Pali–English Dictionary, 26, 31, 33
Pali Text Society, 21–34,
  36
  centenary, 27
Pali Tipitaka, 22
Pali Tipitaka Concordance, 69
Pannavaddho, Ven., 102
Patimokkha, 85
Payne, Francis, 49–50
Practice of Guru Yoga, The, *see*
  Four Foundations
Prajnaparamitas, 45, 46, 140, 142
Precious Human Body, *see* Four
  Great Meditations
Purfurst, William, 102

Rewata Dhamma, Sayadaw U,
  79
Rhys Davids, Mrs, 25
  biography, 35–7
Rhys Davids, Prof. T. W., 18, 22,
  35
  biography, 27–34
'Roaring Silence', The, 119
Roshi Jiyu Kennett, 19, 178–88
Rouse, W.H.D., 25
Royal Danish Academy of Science
  and Letters, 26

Sacred Books of the East, 41
Sacred Ceremony of the Vajra
  Crown, The, 127–9
Saddhatissa, Ven. H., 68, 71, 76
Sakura, 162
Sakya Trizin, HH, 61
Sangha, 89
Sangharakshita, Ven., 19, 160–77
Schloegl, Dr Irmgard, 100
Sesshin, 189–90
Shakhaba, Tsepon, 54
Shasta Abbey, 185–6
'Six Doctrines', 108
Sixty Years of Buddhism in England,
  11
Some Sayings of the Buddha, 42
Soto Zen, 180
  ceremonials, 187
Spirit of Zen, The, 53
Stede, W., 25, 33
Suffering, *see* Four Great
  Meditations
Sunyata, 108, 140, 141
Sutta Pitaka, 22
Suzuki, Dr D. T., 56, 57

Tai Hsu, Ven., 52
Ten Great Precepts, 191–2
Thittila, Ven. Sayadaw U, 102
Thousand Petalled Lotus, The, 163

Three Jewels, The, 164
Throssel Hole Priory, 19, 178–92
Tibet Society, The, 57
Triyana Vardhana Vihara, 161
Trungpa, Ven. Chogyam, 57–9, 106
Turnour, George, 28
'Twelve Principles of Buddhism',
     54

*Universal Responsibility and the
     Good Heart, A*, 152–9

Vajiragnana, Ven. P., 66, 67, 92
Vajrasattva, Meditation on,
     see Four Foundations
Vinaya Pitaka, 22

Vipassana Ten Day Course,
     80

Watts, Allan, 53
Way of Power, The, 126
Webb, Russell, 70–1, 92
Wisdom of the Aryas, The, 45
Woodward, Frank L., 41–3
Working Men's College, 93
World Fellowship of Buddhists,
     12, 56

Zen is Eternal Life, 187–8, 191
Zen Mission Society, 180
Zenji, Rev. Chisan Koho, 180,
     184, 188